Calligraphy
school

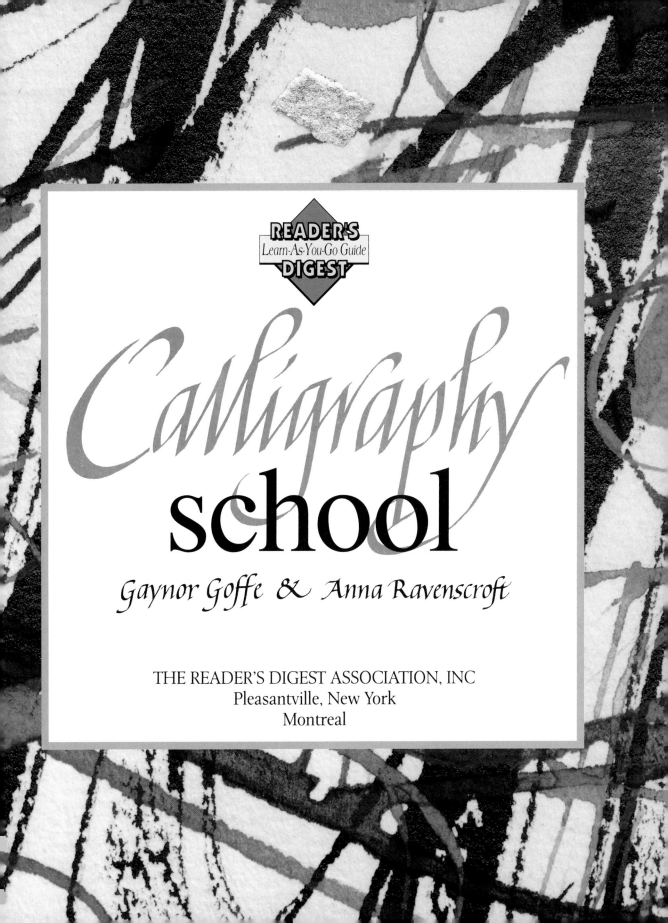

READER'S
Learn-As-You-Go Guide
DIGEST

Calligraphy
school

Gaynor Goffe & Anna Ravenscroft

THE READER'S DIGEST ASSOCIATION, INC
Pleasantville, New York
Montreal

A READER'S DIGEST BOOK

Designed and edited by Quarto Publishing Inc.

Senior Editor *Cathy Meeus*
Senior Art Editor *Penny Cobb*
Designer *Hugh Schermuly*
Picture Managers *Giulia Hetherington, Rebecca Horsewood*
Photographers *Paul Forrester, Chas Wilder*
Illustrators *David Kemp, Ed Stuart*
Editorial Director *Sophie Collins*
Art Director *Moira Clinch*

All calligraphic examples are by the authors except where otherwise stated in the credits on page 176.

The credits that appear on page 176 are hereby made a part of this copyright page.

Library of Congress Cataloging in Publication Data

Goffe, Gaynor
    Calligraphy School : a step-by-step guide to the fine art of lettering / Gaynor Goffe & Anna Ravenscroft.
        p.   cm.
    ISBN 0-89577-524-7
    1. Calligraphy.   I. Ravenscroft, Anna.   II. Title.
    Z43.G599 1993
    745.6'1—dc20   94-2628

Reader's Digest and the Pegasus logo are registered trademarks of The Reader's Digest Association, Inc.

Printed in Singapore

Foreword

There are so many exciting possibilities in calligraphy — from elegant invitations to personalized greeting cards — that it is tempting to try everything. However, once you become familiar with calligraphic principles you soon realize that the skills need to be learned one step at a time.

Written specifically for the beginner, this Learn-as-You-Go Guide is designed to enable the reader to acquire a useful range of working skills in a logical sequence. Throughout the book practical exercises allow the beginner to progressively build a sound body of knowledge, from alphabets to using color.

You do not need a vast store of expensive materials and equipment to learn calligraphy. The first lessons in this book require little more than paper, pencil, and a ruler. Part 2 introduces the use of the broad-nibbed, or edged, pen. Essential confidence-building tech-

niques for handling the pen are explained as well as fundamental principles underlying all calligraphic scripts. The basics of arranging your lettering pleasingly on the page are also discussed in detail.

The main scripts used by calligraphers today are described in Part 3. Mastery of these letterforms will equip you for an interesting range of calligraphy projects. Annotated calligraphic examples and helpful checklists will encourage you to develop a critical eye and to learn from your mistakes. But calligraphy is about more than just letterforms. Effective interpretation of a text is enhanced by the use of color and illustration, and in Part 4 you will find plenty of information on how to make your calligraphic work more decorative.

The final section of this book, the project section, shows some of the uses to which you can put your calligraphy. Each project follows

the development of a piece of calligraphic work step by step from initial idea to finished item. Designed to be within easy reach of the beginning calligrapher, these projects will help you to consolidate the skills you have learned and put them to practical use.

Calligraphy is a demanding but immensely satisfying craft that offers endless creativity.

Gaynor Goffe and Anna Ravenscroft

Contents

3

MASTERING THE LETTERFORMS

4

COLOR AND IMAGE

5

PROJECTS

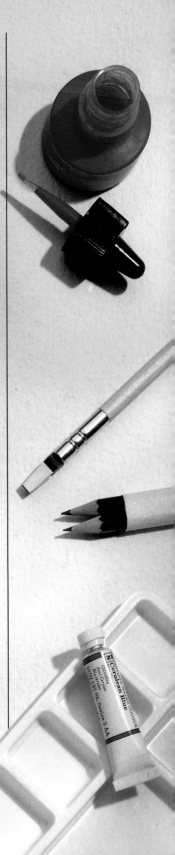

Calligraphy

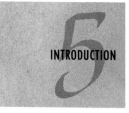
In the United States, and Britain, as well as parts of Europe, recent decades have witnessed a widespread revival of interest in all aspects of calligraphy — in graphic design as a craft and as an artistic medium for self-expression. Calligraphy is now viewed as a tradition with contemporary relevance, rather than an outmoded and archaic practice.

Today's calligraphers have a superb heritage of over 2,000 years of development of the Roman alphabet on which they can draw for their scripts. However experimental you may wish your calligraphy to be, the use of these historical scripts as a basis for your work is vitally important. Such precedents are the roots of modern calligraphy and have a vast wealth of inspiration to offer to every contemporary calligrapher.

THE BEGINNINGS OF CALLIGRAPHY

The earliest examples of the Roman alphabet we use today date from the third century B.C. These early Roman capitals were mostly found incised into stone. Although later there were pen-written Roman capitals, the inscriptional forms — in particular those on Trajan's Column (c. A.D. 114) in Rome — remain unsurpassed as a historical reference.

Other pen-made scripts in use in Roman times include Roman square capitals (quadrata), Rustica (there are also brush-made forms of this script in existence), and Roman cursive — a flowing, everyday script, which was

ROMAN CAPITALS

These incised letters from the Roman Forum are examples of the letterforms from which modern pen-made Roman capitals are derived.

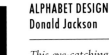

I WENT TO THE WOODS BECAUSE
I WISHED TO LIVE DELIBERATELY
TO FRONT ONLY THE ESSENTIAL FACTS OF LIFE
& SEE IF I COULD NOT LEARN
WHAT IT HAD TO TEACH
AND NOT, WHEN I CAME TO DIE
DISCOVER THAT I HAD NOT LIVED

inscribed into clay and lead tablets and also written on papyrus. This last script was the first in which we see ascenders and descenders.

After the decline of the Roman Empire, the main scripts to be developed were uncials and half uncials, both influenced by Roman precedents. The half uncials found in the English Lindisfarne Gospels and the Irish Book of Kells mark the highpoint of fine writing during the Dark Ages in Europe.

The court of the Emperor Charlemagne was the source of the next major development in scripts. In 789 Charlemagne, seeking to standardize the great variety of scripts in use throughout his domains, decreed that the round bookhand that we now know as Carolingian minuscule be used. The capitals most often used with this script were pen-made, built-up versions of Roman capitals — versals. They were often highly decorated.

I WENT TO THE WOODS
John Nash

This elegant panel of poetry by Henry David Thoreau, written in built-up versal-type capitals, shows the timeless craftsmanship of fine calligraphy. Dimensions: 22" × 9" (56 cm × 23 cm).

BOOK OF KELLS

This supreme example of half uncials, with its delicate ornamentation, was written by Irish scribes in the eighth century.

ALPHABET DESIGN
Donald Jackson

This eye-catching alphabet design shows a delicate tension between elegant gilded classical Roman capitals and the freely written uncial-influenced capitals. Dimensions: 10" × 8" (25.5 cm × 20.5 cm).

The later medieval period saw the evolution of a variety of forms of Gothic (or Black letter) scripts, many of which are, extremely complex and, difficult to read.

THE INTRODUCTION OF ITALIC

The rekindling of interest in classical learning during the Italian Renaissance and the rediscovery of ancient texts led to a revival of Roman capitals and Carolingian minuscules as a basis for formal writing. The Humanist minuscule was an evolution of the latter. The greatest writing landmark of the Renaissance was, however, the development of one of our most beautiful and useful scripts — italic. With its slanting, compressed, and flowing letters, it was the joy of the writing masters and appeared in its myriad variations in the great writing manuals, including those of Arrighi, Palatino, and Tagliente. Its long ascenders and descenders lent themselves to decorative flourishing, while its speed made it practical as a chancery script too.

THE LATE-19th-CENTURY REVIVAL

In the period following the Renaissance, broadpen writing fell into decline, with the growing

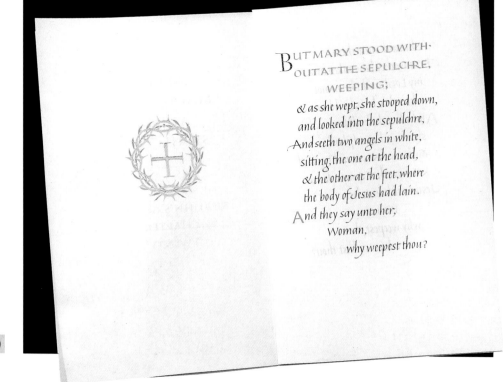

BENTIVOGLIO BOOK OF HOURS

This early 16th century work (above) is written in a rounded Humanistic minuscule. The lavish border decoration is typical of the period.

MANUSCRIPT BOOK
Joan Pilsbury

This elegant and restrained piece of calligraphy (left) uses formal italic, a script that is a direct descendent of the letterforms used in the writing manuals of the 16th century.

COPY No. I. *After* WINCHESTER FORMAL WRITING about 975 A.D.

Et haec scribimus vobis ut gaudeatis, & gaudium vestrum sit plenum.

Et haec est annunciatio, quam audivimus ab eo, & annunciamus vobis: Quoniam Deus lux est, & tenebrae in eo non sunt ullae.

Note: This copy is written with a pen, not printed E.f. 26. August 1919 A.D.

Winchester MS. v. slightly modified.

Heavy Italics based on Winchester MS.

In order that a child may learn how to write well the teaching of handwriting should begin with the practice of a Formal Hand. This Manuscript is written with a BROAD-NIBBED PEN which makes the strokes thick or thin according to the direction in which it moves. The strokes are generally begun downwards or forwards & the letters are formed of several strokes (*the pen being lifted after each stroke*): thus *c* consists of *two* strokes, the first a long curve down, the second a short curve forward. The triangular 'heads' (as for *b* or *d*) are made by *three* strokes; 1st. a short thick curve down, 2nd. a short thin stroke up (*the nib for this stroke being placed on the beginning of the first and slid up to the right*), 3rd. the thick straight *stem* stroke of the letter itself down (*the pen for this stroke not being lifted*).

abcx

Broad-nibbed steel pens and Reeds may be used: Quill pens are very good but require special cutting. — How to cut Quill and Reed pens may be learned from my Handbook "Writing & Illuminating, & Lettering" (*John Hogg, London:* s. 6d. *net*) besides how to make MS. Books and to write in colour. Edward Johnston: *Ditchling, Sussex.*

THIS SHEET IS PUBLISHED BY DOUGLAS PEPLER at HAMPSHIRE HOUSE HAMMERSMITH 1916 A.D.

SAMPLE SHEET
Edward Johnston

Working in the early part of the 20th century, Edward Johnston produced this roundhand script based on the letterforms of the 10th century Ramsey Psalter (see p. 54).

ascendency of pointed-pen copperplate writing. It was not until the late 19th century that the practice of broad-pen calligraphy was revived by William Morris, the key figure in the Arts and Crafts movement. He owned and was influenced by Renaissance manuscripts. Through his manuscript books he engendered an appreciation of the potential of calligraphy in a contemporary setting.

The calligraphic revival was taken further by Edward Johnston, whose pioneering work in the early part of this century involving the study of historical manuscripts resulted in a formal analysis of the letterforms and the principles of broad-pen calligraphy.

In the United States the revival of broad-pen skills was led in the early part of this century by Ernst Detterer, who had studied with Johnston and, independently, John Howard Benson, a Rhode Island stone cutter, and Graham Casey, who, inspired by Johnston's manual, wrote *Elements of Lettering*.

CALLIGRAPHY IN THE MODERN WORLD

Since the middle years of this century, many fine calligraphers have emerged on both sides of the Atlantic. The increasing use of calligraphy in graphic design has provided an additional impetus. The craft is now witnessing a popularity unprecedented in terms of the number of practitioners, not only in the United States and Britain, but also in Australia and throughout Europe. The great variety of cultural traditions in which today's calligraphers work has given contemporary calligraphic work a wonderful breadth and vigor.

Not only does calligraphy have commercial potential, particularly in graphic design, but it is also growing in popularity as an expressive art form and continuing to hold an ever-increasing following as a fine craft. Calligraphy is a skill that is open to all. Whether you have had formal art training or not, there are unlimited possibilities for development along individual paths. Calligraphy brings much creative satisfaction whatever your level of interest and expertise.

POEM
Magnus Aström

This dramatic image inspired by a poem by Yvan Goll (above) shows a successful fusing of illustration and text in a modern context. Dimensions: 24″ × 15″ (61 cm × 38 cm).

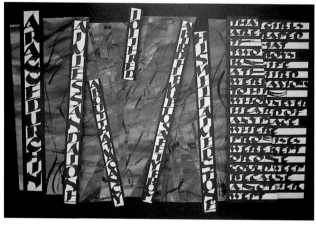

THE SHIELD OF ACHILLES
Florian Kynman

An unusual and exciting rendering of a poem by W. H. Auden. Dimensions: 17½″ × 24″ (95 cm × 61 cm).

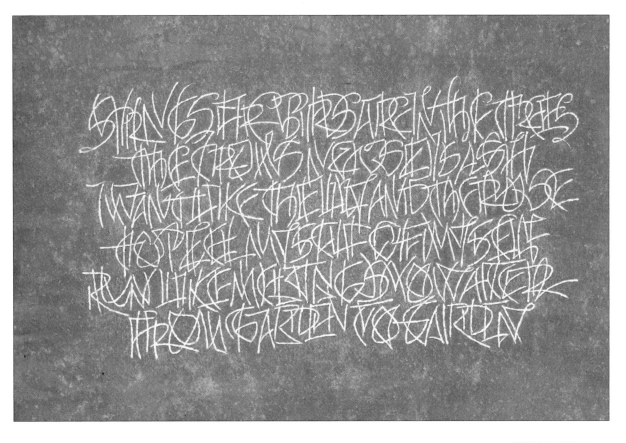

SPRING'S FIREBIRD
Ewan Clayton

In this panel the Roman capitals illustrate how a traditional letterform can be taken in a contemporary direction. Dimensions: 30" × 20" (76 cm × 51 cm).

TEXT BY APOLLINAIRE
Julia Vance

The delicate and striking texture of these capitals, punctuated by subtle use of color, has a powerful presence. Dimensions: 22" × 18" (56 cm × 46 cm).

Laying the foundations

Getting started

The materials for starting calligraphy are simple, inexpensive, and easy to obtain. Pencils, paper, a ruler, and a simple board are all the basic equipment you need. Add to these a few of the items listed opposite. Choosing the right tools and providing yourself with a suitable work surface and comfortable writing position will speed the development of your skills.

Pencils for writing and for ruling lines should be relatively hard: HB or B will give lines that are sharp but easily erased. The points should be fine but not so sharp that they break easily. It helps to begin sharpening with a pencil sharpener or knife and finish with fine sandpaper. You will also need a clean soft eraser for correcting mistakes. For ruling lines, choose a sturdy metal or metal-edged ruler — plastic may chip or warp. In addition, you should obtain a large triangle (with sides about 12″ in length).

Newsprint is an inexpensive choice for pencil practice, or you can use drawing paper — in sheets or a pad. Layout paper, available as single sheets or in pads from art supply stores, is useful for planning and doing creative work. Avoid paper with shiny, textured, or overly rough surfaces, which may affect the flow of your writing.

A board is essential to provide a firm writing surface of adequate size. If the board is too small, it will restrict your arm movement and hamper your writing. Do not be lured at this stage by some of the sophisticated table easels and adjustable boards to be found on the market. Many professional calligraphers produce work of the finest quality without such equipment. Buy a simple board, or make your own (see facing page). This may save money and will ensure the correct size.

PAPER
Inexpensive drawing paper or layout paper is fine for practice. Use good-quality drawing paper for finished work.

SHARPENERS
Pencils must be kept sharp. A pencil sharpener will do the job, as will a craft knife (also useful for cut-and-paste work).

PENCILS
Regular HB or slightly softer, blacker B pencils are widely available.

SANDPAPER
Finish sharpening your pencils with fine sandpaper. Either staple it around a piece of wood, or buy a ready-made sandpaper block from an art store.

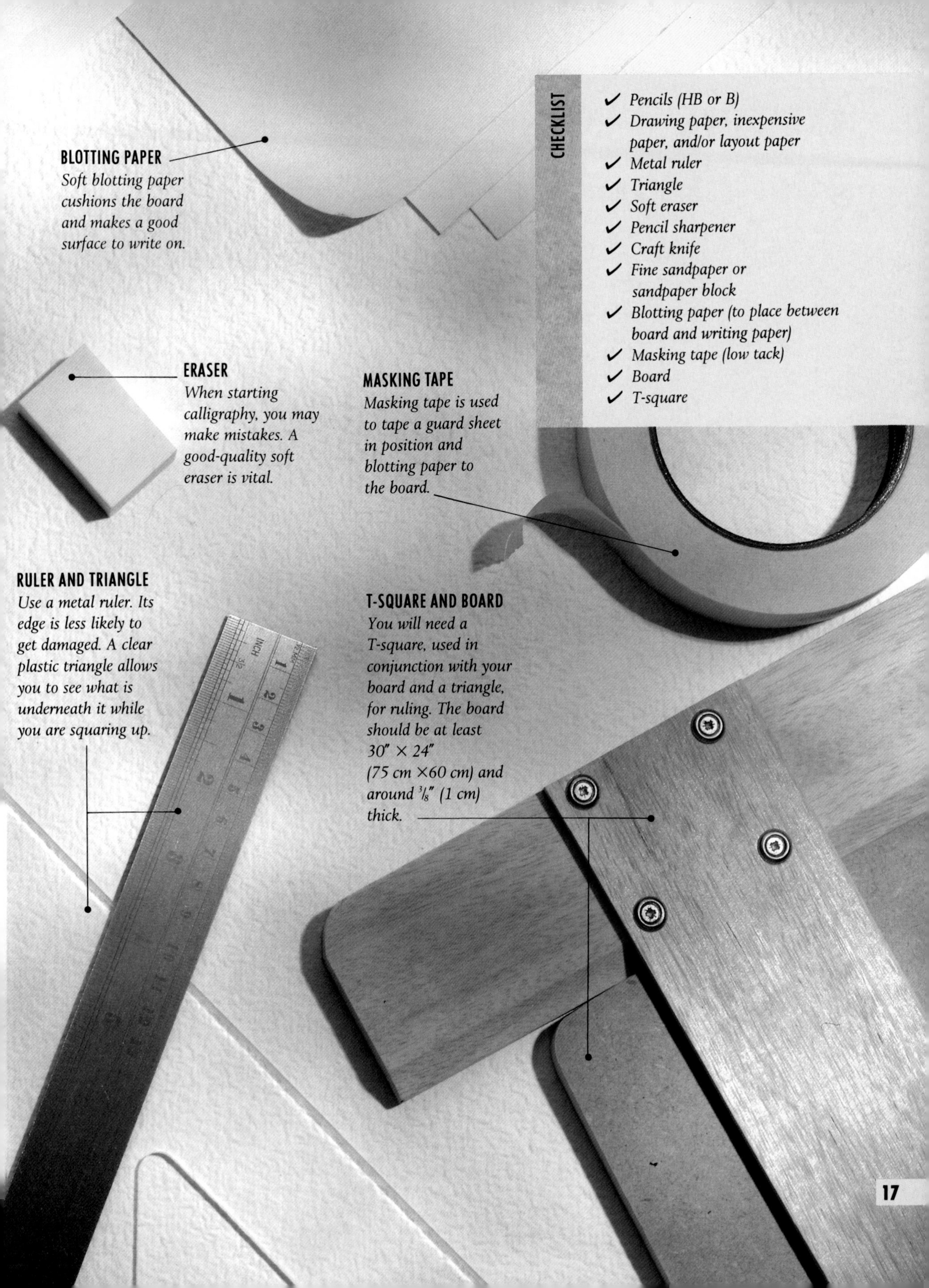

BLOTTING PAPER

Soft blotting paper cushions the board and makes a good surface to write on.

CHECKLIST

✔ Pencils (HB or B)
✔ Drawing paper, inexpensive paper, and/or layout paper
✔ Metal ruler
✔ Triangle
✔ Soft eraser
✔ Pencil sharpener
✔ Craft knife
✔ Fine sandpaper or sandpaper block
✔ Blotting paper (to place between board and writing paper)
✔ Masking tape (low tack)
✔ Board
✔ T-square

ERASER

When starting calligraphy, you may make mistakes. A good-quality soft eraser is vital.

MASKING TAPE

Masking tape is used to tape a guard sheet in position and blotting paper to the board.

RULER AND TRIANGLE

Use a metal ruler. Its edge is less likely to get damaged. A clear plastic triangle allows you to see what is underneath it while you are squaring up.

T-SQUARE AND BOARD

You will need a T-square, used in conjunction with your board and a triangle, for ruling. The board should be at least 30" × 24" (75 cm ×60 cm) and around ³⁄₈" (1 cm) thick.

17

Writing position

Before you even pick up your pencil, it is important to consider writing position. The way you sit is directly reflected in your writing. If your body is tense and angled, your hand and arm are restricted and your writing will not flow. A poor writing position produces awkward and inconsistent letterforms, and this can be very disheartening. You need a posture that optimizes controlled but fluid movement. This means considering the position of your body and the angle of your board (see right).

Writing on an angled board gives you a good overall view of your work as it progresses and will moderate the flow of ink when you come to write with the pen. A raised board also discourages you from leaning over your work. For most writing the board needs to be raised at an angle of 30–45°; you should find the position that suits you best within these guidelines. Ways of raising your board are shown on the facing page.

Use a table and a chair whose relative heights enable you to keep your board at the chosen angle. A table that is too low or a chair that is too high will place you in an uncomfortably high position and will in effect flatten the angle of the board.

CORRECT POSITION

The height of your table and chair should be adjusted to allow you to work with both feet placed side by side on the floor. This will ensure steadiness and reduce tension. By angling your board, you can work without leaning forward.

CROSSED LEGS

The crossed legs and twisted body angle of the person pictured would make it difficult to achieve good writing. This may seem extreme, but it is not unusual to see people assuming this posture unconsciously.

LEANING TOO FAR FORWARD

Avoid the temptation to lean forward, which inhibits arm movement.

HOLDING THE PENCIL

Most calligraphers, whether right- or left-handed, rest the pencil lightly on the first joint of the middle finger and use the thumb and forefinger to guide the pencil point and maintain the required angle to the paper — a steeper one than that usually used for sketching.

LIGHTING CHECKLIST

The type and direction of the light by which you work will affect the quality of your calligraphy. The aim is to have good lighting without shadows cast over your work. Take note of the following guidelines:

- ✔ Good daylight is preferable.
- ✔ Artificial light is best provided by an adjustable desk lamp.
- ✔ "Daylight" bulbs give the best artificial light, especially for work in color.
- ✔ Position your light source to avoid shadows on your work. Light should come from your left if you are right-handed and from your right if you are left-handed.

Right-hander — Light from left, no shadows on work.

Right-hander — Light from right, shadows on work.

RAISING YOUR BOARD

Prop your board at the recommended angle of 30–45° in one of these ways:

A Prop the board against the front edge of the table and rest the base in your lap.

B Place one end of the board on the table and lean the other end on books or covered bricks. Secure the board against the table edge with a thin strip of wood held in place at each end by two small clamps.

C Buy a ready-made designer's drawing board.

D Place your table against a wall and lean your board on the wall at the desired angle. Secure the board against the table edge with a thin strip of wood held in place at each end by two small clamps.

Setting up and ruling up

LAYING THE FOUNDATIONS

Prepare for writing by placing padding between your board and the writing paper. This helps to give a springiness to your writing. You can use any paper, but blotting paper is especially suitable, because its spongy texture gives the right degree of resilience. Tape two or three sheets of this to your board as shown at right.

Keep your work in position and protect it from grease from your hand with a "guard sheet." This is a strip of thin paper — layout paper is ideal — placed across the board and attached on either side with masking tape (see below). Slip your writing sheet under the guard sheet and move it up as you write, leaving the guard sheet fixed in position just beneath each new writing line. This ensures that you are always writing in the best possible position. It is not a good idea to attach the writing sheet to the board, because the change in eye level and in the position of the arm as it moves down a fixed page — particularly toward the bottom where the hand is cramped — causes variations in writing. The area where good writing is most easily achieved is about two-thirds up the board, and the guard sheet is kept just below this in order to maintain a consistently good writing position.

PREPARING THE BOARD
Tape three sheets of blotting paper over your board for the best writing results.

Writing paper

Blotting paper

Board

Masking tape

USING A GUARD SHEET
Tape a guard sheet to your board to protect your work. Do not tape down your writing sheet, so that you can easily adjust its position under the guard sheet as you work.

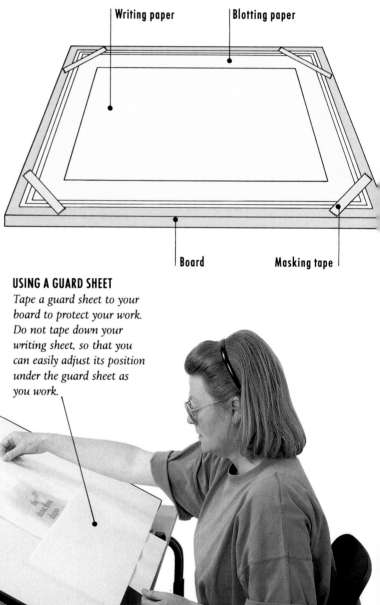

USING A RULER AND TRIANGLE

Calligraphy grids and preruled papers can be slipped under a transparent writing surface for practice in the early stages, but it is a good idea to get into the habit of ruling your own lines as soon as possible. Preruled lines can be restricting and may not give accurate results. To guide your writing you will need to rule straight and accurately spaced lines. Using a triangle and a ruler will help to keep the lines parallel. The photographs below show you what to do. An alternative is to use a T-square to draw your writing lines. Align the end of the T-square with the left edge of your board and slide it up or down to the required position.

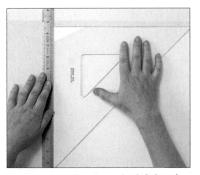

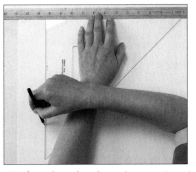

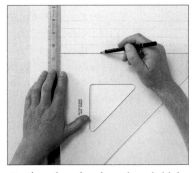

1 *Place the ruler along the left-hand edge of the paper. Hold the triangle against the ruler, and slide it up to the top edge of the paper. If the top edge of the triangle does not align with the paper, the paper is not square and should be trimmed accordingly.*

2 *Place the ruler along the top edge of the paper. Slide the top edge of the triangle along the ruler until the left-hand edge of the triangle is in the position in which you wish to place your left margin. Lightly rule the margin in pencil.*

3 *Place the ruler along the ruled left margin. Slide the triangle down the ruler until the top edge is in the position in which you want to place your first writing line. Lightly rule a line. Continue to move the triangle down the ruler and rule as many lines as you want.*

LINE SPACING AND MARGINS

A block of writing looks better if it has a margin around it to set it off. It is usual to have an equal measurement at the top and sides (A), with double this (2 × A) at the bottom margin.

The distance between writing lines (interline space) is determined by the x height of the letters. This is the height of the body of a lowercase (minuscule) letter, excluding ascenders or descenders (tops and tails on letters such as b and p) (see "Letter height," p. 24). Sufficient space must be left between writing lines, however, to accommodate ascenders and descenders without their becoming entangled. A distance three times the x height from baseline to baseline is usually best when using lowercase letters.

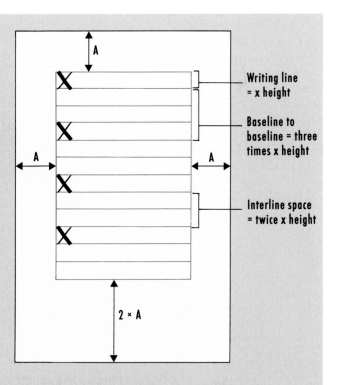

Writing line = x height

Baseline to baseline = three times x height

Interline space = twice x height

A basic alphabet

For your first calligraphy, work with a simple but interesting script. The lowercase alphabet used here, based on the circle, is an excellent starting point and, when written rhythmically, forms a useful and attractive script. This script is chosen largely because of its legibility to the modern reader, accustomed to the square capitals and rounded lowercase letters of printed Roman type. The clear relationship between the letterforms of this basic script makes it an ideal introduction to the pleasures of calligraphy and one that forms the basis of all calligraphic work.

The key features of the basic alphabet, in its pencil-drawn form, are shown on the facing page. It is a good idea to look at these before you begin writing to give yourself an overview of the characteristics of this script.

The best way to learn any script is to practice the letters first in pencil in their skeleton form — without thicks and thins. This enables you to establish and understand the letter proportions and shapes and their relationship to one another. Getting the feel of the script and fixing the basic letterforms firmly in your mind at this stage will make the use of the broad-nibbed pen easier and more successful.

QUOTATION FROM HAMLET
Gareth Colgan

Here a basic (roundhand) script has been written with energy and rhythm to produce a dramatic interpretation of the text. Even the most straightforward of letterforms has the potential to produce calligraphic work of great quality. Dimensions: 13" × 23" (33 cm × 58.5 cm).

CLAUDIUS
O, my offence is rank, it smells to heaven,
It hath the primal eldest curse upon't,
A brother's murder! Pray can I not,
Though inclination be as sharp as will.
My stronger guilt defeats my strong intent,
And like a man to double business bound,
I stand in pause where I should first begin,
And both neglect. What if this cursèd hand
Were thicker than itself with brother's blood,
Is there not rain enough in the sweet heavens
To wash it white as snow? Whereto serves mercy
But to confront the visage of offence?
And what's in prayer but this two-fold force,
To be forestallèd ere we come to fall.
Or pardoned being down? then I'll look up...
My fault is past. but O, what form of prayer
Can serve my turn? 'Forgive me my foul murder'?
That cannot be since I am still possessed
Of those effects for which I did the murder,
My crown, mine own ambition, and my queen:
May one be pardoned and retain the offence?
In the corrupted currents of this world
Offence's gilded hand may shove by justice,
And oft 'tis seen the wicked prize itself
Buys out the law. But 'tis not so above,
There is no shuffling, there the action lies
In his true nature, and with ourselves
to ...

REMORSELESS LECHEROUS
TREACHEROUS KINDLESS
VILLAIN O VENGEANCE!

... compelled
Even the teeth and forehead of our faults
To give in evidence. What then? What rests?
Try what repentance can — what can it not?
Yet what can it when one can not repent?
O wretched state! O bosom black as death!
O limèd soul that struggling to be free,
Art more engaged; help, angels! Make assay,
Bow stubborn knees, & heart with strings of steel
Be soft as sinews of the new-born babe —
All may be well.

HAMLET: WILLIAM SHAKESPEARE

GEOMETRIC FORMS

Basic script letterforms are founded on the concept of a circle within a square, as shown in the diagrams on the right. You do not need to draw the letters geometrically, but an awareness of these underlying principles will help you understand the structure and proportions of the letterforms and provide a useful reference when you are writing the letters freehand in the exercises that come later.

Although each letter of the alphabet is different, groups of letters share common elements and the same strokes frequently recur. The quickest and easiest way to learn, therefore, is to practice letters in groups of similar formation and width. Most basic script letters are three-quarters the width of the circle on which they are founded (see right), and they belong to four formation groups (next page). The letters in the formation group diagrams are the same size as those you will be writing. It may be helpful to trace them once or twice first. Numerals and arrows show the order in which you should write your strokes and the direction in which to move your pencil. When you come to writing the letters freehand, modifications will be needed to c, d, e, and x, for aesthetic reasons. These are indicated in the skeleton alphabet (p. 26). Have a look at this and refer once more to the geometric diagrams before you begin to practice the formation groups shown on the next page.

Straight-sided arched letters: n, m, h, r, a, plus i and l. These are three-quarters width, except m (which is double this width), and i and l (which are single strokes with no substantial width).

Circular letters: g, c, e, d, q, b, p, o. These are seven-eighths width, except the fully circular o and g (which is based on a smaller o).

Letters containing diagonals: k, v, w, y, x, z. These are three-quarters width, except w (which is double this width).

Letters with related top and tail curves: f, s, j. These are three-quarter width.

Straight-sided letters with related base curve: t, u. These are three-quarter width.

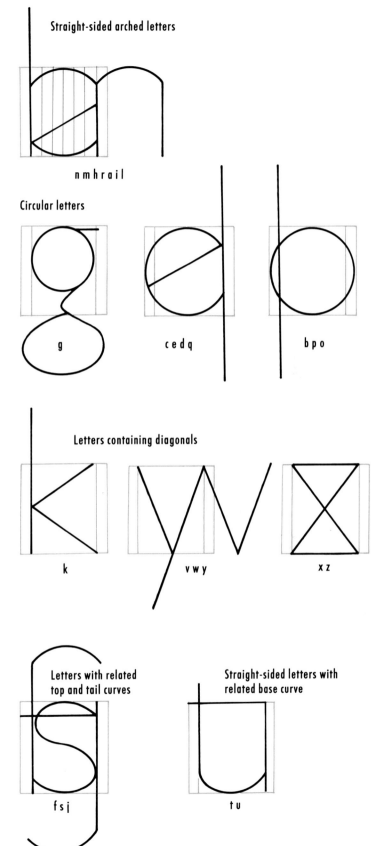

Straight-sided arched letters

n m h r a i l

Circular letters

g   c e d q   b p o

Letters containing diagonals

k   v w y   x z

Letters with related top and tail curves

f s j

Straight-sided letters with related base curve

t u

LETTER HEIGHT

Before practicing even the most basic script, you will need to have some understanding of the size and proportions of the letters. For a lowercase script the key measurement is the x height. This is the height of the main part, or body, of the letter, excluding ascenders and descenders (see right). The height of capital scripts is defined by the overall height of the letters. For most of the exercises in this section, the letters should be written to an x height of ½" (13 mm). Ascenders and descenders are slightly shorter.

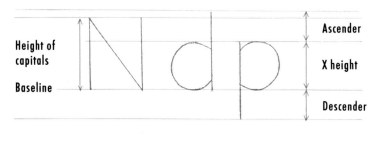

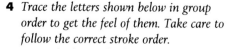

LETTER FORMATION GROUPS

Before attempting to write a basic script with a broad-nibbed pen, practice the formation groups in pencil as shown below.

1 *Using an HB pencil, rule your practice sheet with lines ½" (13 mm) apart.*

2 *Leave two blank lines between each writing line or arrange the groups as shown in the model to avoid the collision of ascenders and descenders.*

3 *Refer to the diagrams (p. 23) to remind yourself how the letters relate to the square and the circular o. The alphabet on p. 26 gives further information about the forms of individual letters.*

4 *Trace the letters shown below in group order to get the feel of them. Take care to follow the correct stroke order.*

5 *Write the letters freehand, group by group, in HB pencil. Repeat each group several times before moving on to the next.*

6 *Check the letters against the model after each writing. You will use the same sequence when you write with the pen.*

7 *Draw the letters firmly. Correct the shapes as you go, erasing if necessary. Your aim is to get an understanding of the structure and relationship of the letter shapes. This is bound to entail a number of attempts.*

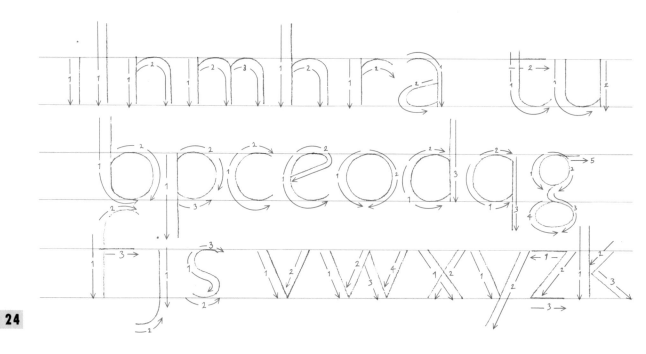

ALTERNATIVE LETTERFORMS

The letterforms shown on the previous page are the standard ones for the basic script. However, some letters can be rendered in a different way. The choice is a matter for the individual calligrapher. Some common alternative forms are shown at right with guidance as to stroke order and direction. Try these when you feel confident with the standard alphabet.

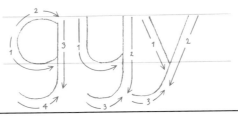

SPACING AND THE RULE OF THREE

The aim of spacing in any script is to make the areas of space within and between letters appear equal. If all letters were straight-sided, this would be easy — you could simply measure the same amount of space between each of them. But because letterforms vary, you need to be aware of the spacing needs of different combinations of letters.

This means thinking about the area inside each letter — the counter space — as well as the white area created around the letter itself. In practical terms, to achieve even spacing, a curved letter should be placed closer to a straight-sided letter than another straight-sided form is, and two adjacent curved letters should be placed closest of all.

Spacing patterns for each script can be established with the aid of a key diagram (see right). Using this diagram, you can practice and verify the amount of space needed to achieve a balanced effect.

A helpful way to check your spacing is with the "Rule of Three." Look at the first three letters in your writing (of the alphabet or a word) and see whether the space on either side of the middle letter appears equal. Then, looking at the last two letters of that trio and the following letter, verify the spacing on either side of the new middle letter. Continue in the same fashion until you have checked the entire alphabet or word.

You can learn the principles of even spacing between differently shaped letters by practicing the following exercise.

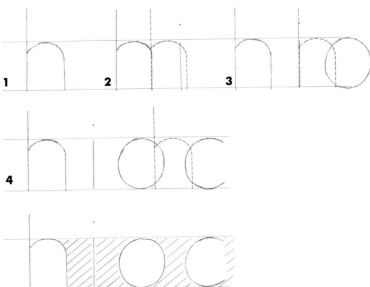

1 Rule lines in pencil ½" (12 mm) apart. Copy the h i o c diagram above in pencil, using the following guidelines.

2 Write the h, ensuring that it is the correct width because it will determine the spacing pattern. Place an i next to it, slightly closer than the width of the h counter (the space inside the h).

3 Write an o slightly closer to the i. To maintain the appearance of equal space, adjacent straight-sided and curved letters need to be closer than a pair of straight-sided letters.

4 Place the c even nearer to the o, because adjacent curved letters let in additional space between them at top and bottom.

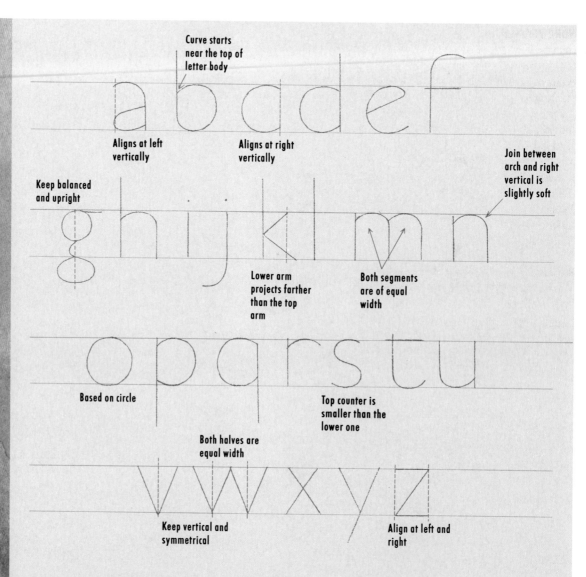

Curve starts near the top of letter body

Aligns at left vertically

Aligns at right vertically

Join between arch and right vertical is slightly soft

Keep balanced and upright

Lower arm projects farther than the top arm

Both segments are of equal width

Based on circle

Top counter is smaller than the lower one

Both halves are equal width

Keep vertical and symmetrical

Align at left and right

Use the knowledge acquired through practicing letter groups and spacing to write and space the full skeleton basic alphabet. Don't be held back by faults in letterforms and spacing on the first attempt, but consider where you could make improvements before you try again. Work on lines ruled ½″ (13 mm) apart and copy the alphabet in sections (a-f, g-n, o-u, v-z), spacing the letters as evenly as possible.

CHECKLIST
- ✔ Letters should not slant.
- ✔ Letter bodies (except g) should fill the space between lines.
- ✔ b, d, p, and q have curves based on the circular o and should contain an equal area within the counter.
- ✔ The arches of h, m, n, a, and r should reflect the circular o.
- ✔ Base curves of t and u reflect the circular o.
- ✔ Crossbars of t and f are at the level of the x height.

WORD PRACTICE

The best way to get used to spacing is to check and rewrite the same few words. Begin with words containing mainly straight-sided letters, which are spaced equidistantly. Concentrated practice with repeated letter combinations will not only help you achieve even spacing but develop your ability to judge and improve your spacing with unfamiliar texts. For spacing between words, you should leave room for an o of the script being written, so in this case make the space between your words the width of a basic script o.

1 *Rule lines ¹/₂" (13 mm) apart.*

2 *Write the words shown.*

3 *Check the letterforms and spacing and repeat as necessary to correct any errors.*

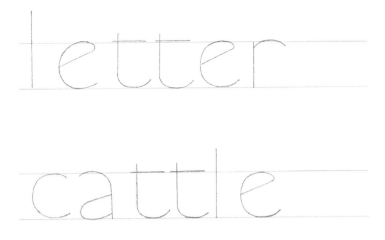

Using colored pencils

Even at this early stage in your knowledge of calligraphy, you can aim to produce attractive finished work. Try using colored pencils for uncomplicated projects such as the labels for storage jars shown here. The basic script with its clear and legible letterforms is ideal for this purpose. A simple decorative border provides the finishing touch.

1 *Rule the writing lines to the desired height, and write the words in pencil to allow letterforms and spacing to be checked and corrected if necessary.*

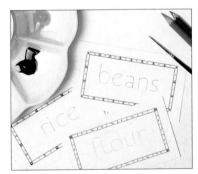

2 *The final versions, written in colored pencil, have borders worked in gouache. Care is needed to ensure the correct placement of the border around the text.*

The basics of broad-pen calligraphy

Tools and materials

THE BASICS OF BROAD-PEN CALLIGRAPHY

The increasing popularity of calligraphy has brought with it a huge range of writing tools and materials. The variety may seem confusing at first, but bear in mind that the only additions to your basic equipment (pp. 16–17) that you really need are pen and ink.

The essential tool for most pen-written calligraphy is a pen with a broad-edged nib. That is why calligraphy is sometimes termed "the art of the broad-nibbed pen." To write accurate strokes you have to keep the entire edge of the nib consistently in contact with the paper. This can feel awkward at first, and it may help to spend a little time practicing with a double pencil (below left), whose twin points produce the same effect as the broad nib with an outline form. Alternatively, you can use a broad-edged carpenter's pencil (below right), sharpened to a chisel shape, which reproduces the action of the broad pen even more directly. Choose a medium to soft grade, or the type made for drawing, which will not need to be pressed too hard to make a mark.

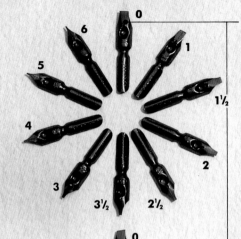

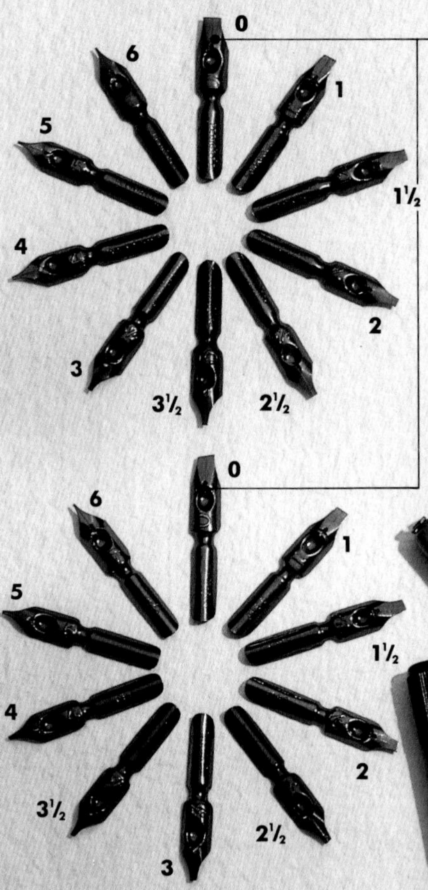

NIBS

Mitchell's roundhand nibs are made in sizes 0–6, including some half-sizes. The lower the number, the broader the nib. Other makes use different sizing systems (see "Checking your nib size," p. 33). Left-oblique nibs, for left-handed calligraphers are shown below left.

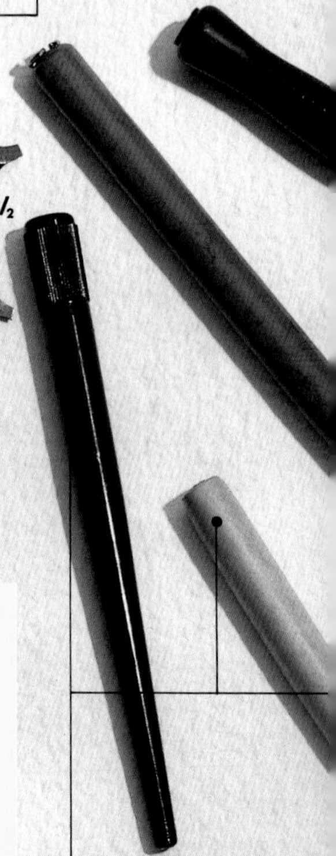

DOUBLE PENCILS

Make your own double pencils by binding together two HB pencils with a rubber band or masking tape. The points can be brought closer by shaving one side of each pencil with a sharp craft knife — keeping the cut areas level and not exposing the lead — before binding them firmly using masking tape with the points aligned. (For left-handers, the right point should be slightly higher.)

CARPENTER'S PENCIL

A flat carpenter's pencil can be sharpened into the shape of a broad nib. This is very useful for practicing weighted letterforms.

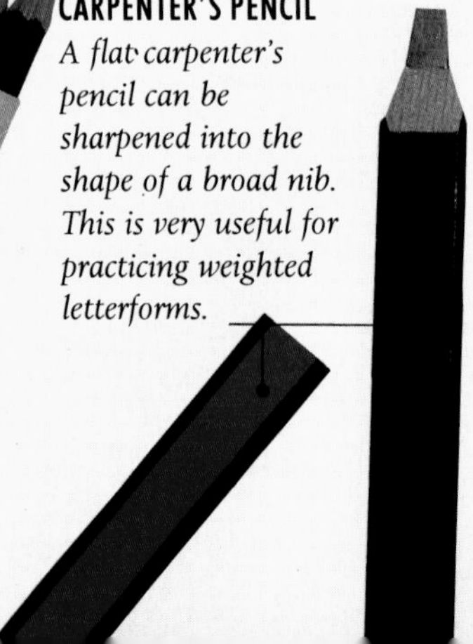

PENHOLDERS

Some calligraphers find rounded penholders more comfortable to hold than faceted ones.

FOUNTAIN PENS
With their large-capacity reservoirs, fountain pens are useful for the beginner, who can practice without constantly having to refill the pen. Fountain-pen sets come with a range of nib sizes.

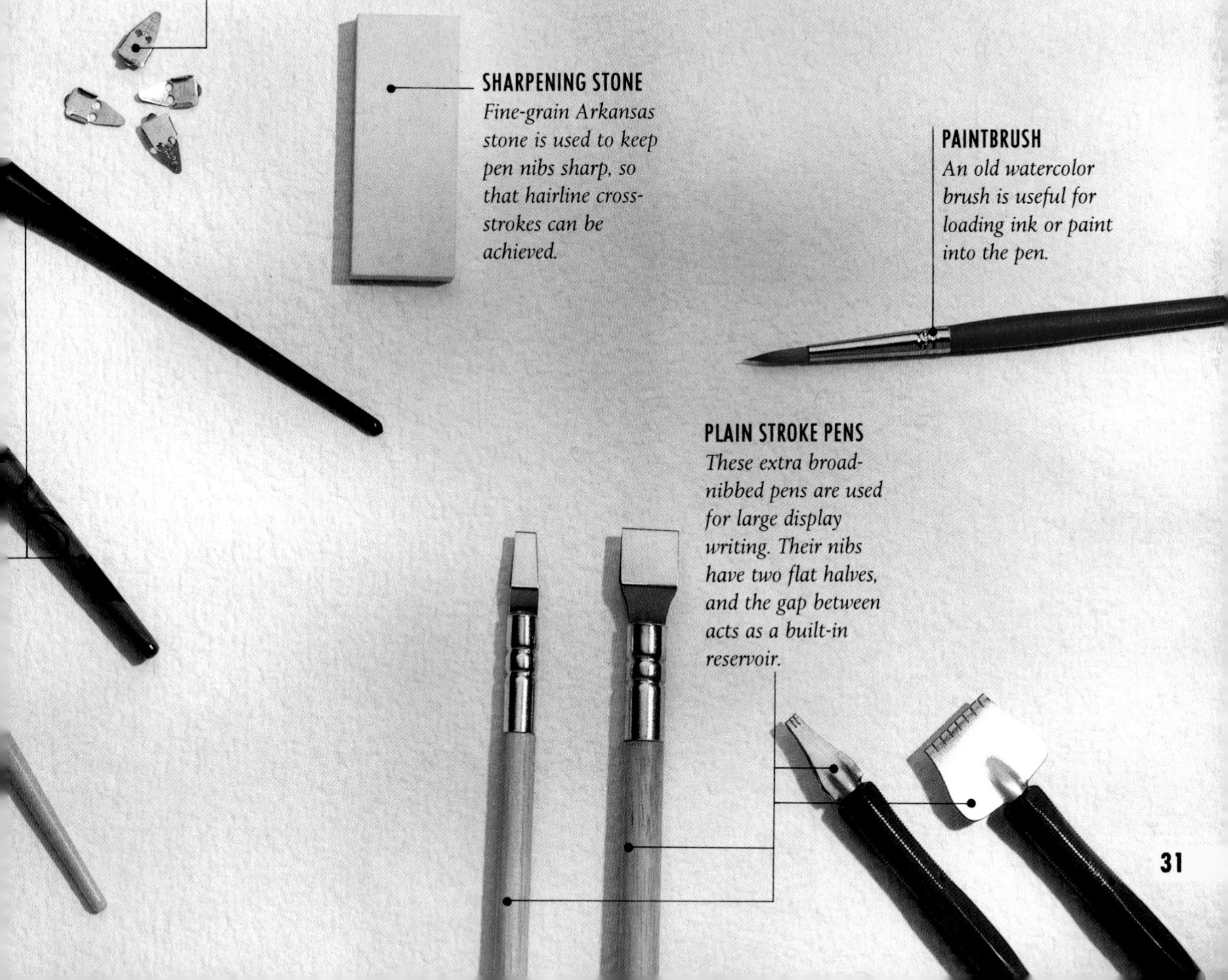

RESERVOIRS
Most small clip-on reservoirs fit on the back of the nibs used with assembled pens.

SHARPENING STONE
Fine-grain Arkansas stone is used to keep pen nibs sharp, so that hairline cross-strokes can be achieved.

PAINTBRUSH
An old watercolor brush is useful for loading ink or paint into the pen.

PLAIN STROKE PENS
These extra broad-nibbed pens are used for large display writing. Their nibs have two flat halves, and the gap between acts as a built-in reservoir.

The many varieties of broad-nibbed pen fall into two main categories: the pen you assemble (also known as a dip pen), consisting of a holder and a steel nib, usually with a reservoir that fits above or beneath it; and the fountain pen with a built-in reservoir. The function of the reservoir is to extend the flow of ink by storing it and feeding it steadily to the nib edge. Fountain pens have large-capacity reservoirs, which do not need to be constantly refilled. They are useful when practicing and for traveling. They can be purchased as a set that includes interchangeable nibs of different sizes. A fountain pen with a squeeze- or piston-fill reservoir is preferable to a cartridge refill, which limits changes of ink color. The pen should be kept meticulously clean to allow the ink to flow freely.

Continued on page 33 ▷

31

Assembling the pen

One of the advantages of assembling a pen is that you can adjust it to suit your individual requirements. Dismantling, cleaning, and reassembling it regularly also help you become well acquainted with your writing instrument. The assembled pen shown here is the standard pen used for teaching the scripts throughout this book.

1 *Ease the nib into the holder. Avoid putting pressure on the writing edge. Slide the nib in as far as possible. It should fit closely to the holder's neck.*

2 *With a new nib, be sure to remove the protective lacquer coating. Plunge it into hot water, or hold it briefly in a flame and then cool it in cold water.*

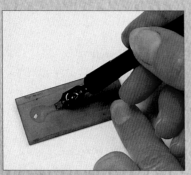

3 *Place a sharpening stone on a flat surface and lubricate it with water. Place the nib at 30°, with the top toward the stone and the back of the nib facing you.*

4 *Keeping the nib at 30°, move it across the stone 10–12 times. Check the sloping edge of the nib under a magnifying glass and sharpen it with the top of the nib facing you until it is even.*

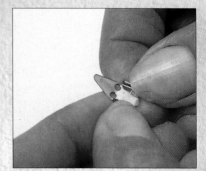

5 *It may be necessary to fit the reservoir by first loosening the side flaps with slight pressure from your finger and thumb so that it can slide easily onto the nib.*

6 *The reservoir should make just enough contact to prevent it from falling off. It must not grip the nib so tightly that it distorts the writing edge.*

7 *The reservoir should be positioned about 1/8" (3 mm) from the writing edge or slightly closer on smaller nib sizes.*

8 *If the reservoir is too far forward, it will catch the paper and drag ink across the surface; if too far back, it will not supply ink to the writing edge.*

Calligraphic felt-tip pens with broad, chisel-shaped tips are useful for planning layout ideas, but are not normally used for finished work, where accuracy is essential.

You can get good results from either fountain or assembled pens, and it is important to choose the type of pen with which you feel most comfortable. Sooner or later, however, you will probably want to try the pen-holder, nib, and reservoir that you assemble yourself. This is because of the flexibility it offers with its vast range of nibs. It is also easier to change color and to wash nibs, and you can regularly check all the working parts.

HANDMADE PENS

It is easy to make your own pens from a fine piece of bamboo. Such pens can produce interesting and individual lettering effects.

Cleaning the pen

Taking care of your tools can become an enjoyable part of the whole craft, not a chore. A pen must be kept clean to perform well. Nibs left with ink or paint drying in their recesses will clog and rust. Rust will also develop on penholders left to soak in water with their nibs attached. When writing is finished, the penholder, nib, and reservoir need to be separated, washed, and dried.

1 *Ease the reservoir off the nib and soak in a bowl of lukewarm soapy water. If it is stuck, do not force it. This may damage the nib. Soak it first to loosen any dried ink.*

2 *Dip an old toothbrush in the lukewarm water, and gently scrub both sides of the nib and reservoir.*

3 *Immediately after washing, dry the nib and reservoir with a cotton rag. Do not use tissues, which leave fibers.*

CHECKING YOUR NIB SIZE

Throughout this book the nib sizes quoted refer to Mitchell's roundhand nibs, which are widely used by calligraphers. If you are using a different brand, you will need to convert these sizes to those of your nib. A simple way of doing this is to hold each of your nibs against the size checker below to determine which Mitchell's size it most closely matches.

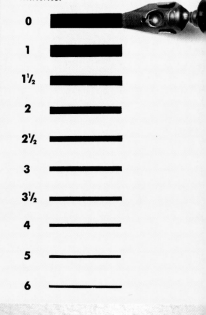

0
1
1½
2
2½
3
3½
4
5
6

Inks and paints

THE BASICS OF BROAD-PEN CALLIGRAPHY

To produce the sharp strokes that characterize calligraphy, your pen and your ink must be compatible. The inks used by medieval scribes (often composed of lampblack — a kind of soot — mixed with gum and water) were efficient and durable, as surviving manuscripts testify. But inks that had been suitable for quills frequently corroded metal pens, and during the 19th century alternative inks were developed. Some calligraphers continue to make inks from old recipes for creative purposes, but nowadays there are a great number of prepared inks from which to choose, offering a variety of properties.

It is fun to experiment with inks once you have gained confidence, but for now there are only two factors to consider. The ink must flow smoothly and be an intense black, even when dry. Some inks appear black at the time of writing but dry to a disappointing gray. For smooth flow, the ink must be nonwaterproof.

You can buy nonwaterproof ink ready for use or in a thick solution to be diluted with water. Use distilled water, not water from the faucet, or the ink will deteriorate. Remember to keep the lid on, so that the ink does not dry around the top of the bottle and flake into the liquid. Always shake the bottle or stir the ink before starting to write, and if you write for a long period, stir the ink occasionally.

The introduction of color in the pen strokes or background opens up a vast range of creative possibilities. The methods used are easily within the reach of the beginner. The paints generally used by calligraphers are artists' watercolors, gouache (an opaque form of watercolor), and some liquid acrylics.

INKS
Both the black calligraphers' ink you use and the colored inks should be nonwaterproof, as the shellac in waterproof inks can clog the pen.

LIQUID ACRYLICS
Only water-based paints are suitable for use in the pen. Liquid acrylics mix better than acrylics from a tube.

PALETTE
Mix your paint on a palette. Use distilled water if you plan to store the paint.

If you fill your pen by dipping it directly into the ink or paint, it is difficult to control the amount of liquid in the reservoir, and you may get drips on your paper. It is therefore advisable to use a brush to feed ink or paint directly into the reservoir. Always make sure there is no ink or paint on the upper surface of the nib.

USING INK

Fill a medium-size paintbrush with ink. With the brush in one hand and the pen in the other, feed the ink in from one side between the nib and the reservoir. A dropper may be used instead of a brush to load ink into the reservoir.

USING PAINT

1 *Squeeze out about ¼" (6 mm) of paint or gouache. Add water and blend thoroughly with a soft paintbrush until the mixture is the consistency of ink.*

2 *Load the reservoir with the paint using a brush.*

3 *Test the paint flow on a piece of scrap paper. If the paint is too thin, the color will not be strong enough. If the paint is too thick, it will clog the pen.*

4 *Make sure you mix enough paint to complete the job. A change to a new batch of color halfway through is likely to show.*

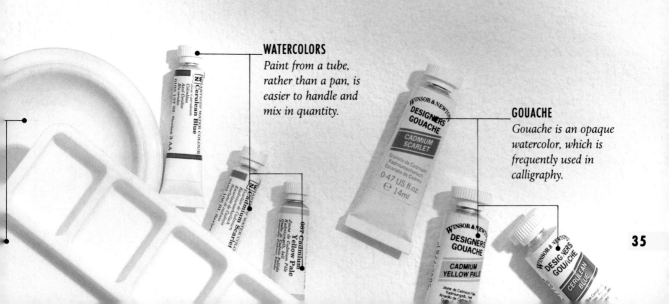

WATERCOLORS
Paint from a tube, rather than a pan, is easier to handle and mix in quantity.

GOUACHE
Gouache is an opaque watercolor, which is frequently used in calligraphy.

Paper

Paper makes a great contribution to the mood, direction, and success of the work produced on it. By getting to know some of the many types of paper available and how they behave with the nib, you can increase the accuracy of your writing and the beauty of your designs.

Medieval manuscripts were written on parchment or its finer-quality counterpart, vellum — both durable surfaces made from animal skin. Printing brought about the development of paper made from vegetable fibers. Today calligraphers choose their papers from three main categories: handmade, mold-made, and machine-made.

Handmade papers are made by dipping a mesh-covered frame, known as a mold, into a solution of fibers. These are held in place on the mold by another frame called a deckle, which gives its name to the distinctive wavy edges of a handmade sheet. The same materials are used to produce mold-made papers, but the process is speeded by a cylinder-mold machine, which produces the paper as a continuous roll. The quality of mold-made paper is close to that of handmade sheets, but there are only two deckle edges, and machine production usually makes them less expensive.

Machine-made papers are mass-produced. Their main advantage is their low cost. Many machine-made papers are suitable for calligraphy and artwork. Machine-made papers are especially useful for practicing and planning, so that you do not have to worry about wasting expensive paper.

CHOOSING PAPERS

When choosing paper, you need to consider its weight and its surface. The weight, which indicates the thickness, is especially important

PAPER SAMPLES

Build a collection of samples of papers that interest you, storing them in a folder. Remember to label each paper, and annotate it with observations on how it affects nib movement and how it interacts with ink and paint.

after wash

Becoming familiar with different types of paper will enable you to choose the best surface for your work. Knowing the cause of paper problems can be helpful.

SURFACE TOO ROUGH

Ink flow is impeded and it is difficult to guide the nib steadily and smoothly.

SURFACE TOO SLIPPERY

The nib cannot be controlled. Ink builds up on the surface and may run into lower lines.

UNSIZED, OR WATERLEAF, PAPER

Absorbs ink or paint like blotting paper.

TEXTURED PAPER

Surface bumps may distort writing, and may contain hairs that are picked up by the nib.

UNEVEN SIZING

This causes the letters to "bleed" in patches.

GREASY SURFACE

This resists the writing medium. Grease spots can cause the same problem.

Cold-pressed paper

Hot-pressed paper

Pastel paper

Mold-made pastel paper

Cover paper

when using painted backgrounds (see pp. 124–7). Surfaces are graded as hot-pressed, cold-pressed, or rough, according to the processes used to dry the paper. Porosity is affected by the addition to the paper of a gluey substance known as size. Unsized or poorly sized papers allow ink or paint to spread, or "bleed," into the fibers, and too much size can make the surface too resistant. Test a paper's suitability by trying it out with the pen: if the surface drags or catches in the nib, or the ink bleeds, it is probably unsuitable. However, certain surface difficulties can be overcome (see "Surface preparation," below). Highly coated, glossy papers should be rejected; the ink is likely to stand in blobs on the surface.

SELECTING THE TOP SIDE

Papers sometimes have different surfaces on different sides. The top side usually has a smoother finish. With watermarked papers, you can find out which is the top side by holding the paper up to the light and looking for the watermark. If it reads properly, the top side is toward you.

SURFACE PREPARATION

You can improve writing sharpness on porous or greasy papers by sealing the surface with a special fixative spray or with gum sandarac, a traditional material favored by many calligraphers. Gum sandarac is bought in crystals. Grind these to a fine powder with a mortar and pestle. Place the powder in a square of clean fine white cotton, gather the corners of the square together, and tie at the neck to form a little bundle. Shake this gently to allow a light dusting of powder to fall on your paper. Too much will mar the writing, so take care to blow away any excess.

Holding the pen

It is important to establish a way of holding the pen that allows a firm and steady grip, but that also enables you easily to change the pen angle when needed. Most calligraphers rest the pen on the first joint of the middle finger and use the thumb and forefinger to guide the pen and maintain its angle. This approach is used for any broad-edged writing instrument.

Pen angle problems are more marked in the early stages of learning. A flatter angle to the writing line is more natural than a steep one, so you will need to check the angle constantly at first. You also need to ensure that your pen holder is held at the correct angle to your writing surface to facilitate smooth writing — 40°-60° is best.

CHANGING PEN ANGLE

The simplest way of altering the angle of the nib with minimum disruption to writing flow is to roll the pen between your thumb and forefinger without altering the position of your hand. In the illustrations you will see how the angle of the penholder held in your hand moves in a 90° arc as you change the angle of the nib from 0° through 45° to 90°.

0°

45°

90°

ANGLE OF PEN TO BOARD
Establish an angle of 40°–60° between your pen and board for best results. In this picture you can see how the heel of the hand rests on the board to ensure stability.

RIGHT-HANDED
Most right-handers find it easy to adopt a grip in which the pen is held lightly but firmly between the thumb and forefinger and rests on the first joint of the middle finger.

HINTS FOR LEFT-HANDERS

For most scripts the strokes are pull rather than push strokes — that is, the pen is pulled across the paper instead of being pushed. These standard stroke directions are aimed at right-handers, who form the majority of the population. In order to follow the correct stroke direction, left-handed calligraphers cannot simply use a mirror image of the right-handed writing positions but have to adopt alternative positions for their hands and arms.

Left-handed calligraphers have discovered many ways of overcoming this difficulty, but for beginners the underarm position shown right is considered most effective. This position enables strokes to be the same as for right-handers, and the work can be viewed from a regular perspective. Penholder and nib are aligned in a similar way to the right-handed pen — an obvious advantage when learning from a right-handed teacher or right-handed examples. However, this position may not suit all left-handed calligraphers. Alternative positions are shown in the panel below right. You may need to experiment with different methods before you find the solution that is best for you.

A more general difficulty encountered by left-handers is achieving and maintaining a steep-enough pen angle to the paper. Some people solve this by turning the paper up to the left, but this may disturb the writing of verticals and constant slants. Oblique nibs (shown on page 30) can help left-handers to achieve accurate angles.

Do not be discouraged if it takes a little time to find a way of writing comfortably; many successful calligraphers are left-handed, and there are satisfactory solutions to most individual difficulties. Discussions with other left-handers and watching demonstrations may help. It is important to remember, however, that most beginning calligraphy problems are common to both left- and right-handers.

UNDERARM POSITION FOR LEFT-HANDERS

At the wrist, turn the left hand as far as possible to the left in order to place the nib on the paper at the correct angle. It may help to slant your paper down to the right. Encourage free arm movement by placing the paper slightly to the left of your body and writing from this position. It helps if you work on an extra-wide board with a guard sheet across the full width, so that you can move your work to the left as you write.

ALTERNATIVE LEFT-HAND POSITIONS

If for any reason the underarm position does not suit you, try one of these alternatives.

HOOK POSITION

Place your hand above the writing line in a "hook" position by flexing the wrist downward. Then, after placing the nib on the paper at the desired angle, move the nib in the direction of the stroke. It may help to slant the paper slightly to the left.

VERTICAL POSITION

In this method the paper is placed at 90° to the horizontal and you work from top to bottom instead of from left to right. This enables strokes to be rendered as for right-handers, but the unusual angle may make it difficult to judge the letterforms as you work.

Making a mark

When you begin to write with the broad-nibbed pen, one of the first questions that arises is how to encourage or how to control the ink flow. Gentle pressure on the nib and small pulling strokes on a spare piece of paper will usually get the pen started. If not, check that the reservoir is in contact with the nib, that the fit is not too tight, and that it is close enough to the edge of the nib (see "Assembling the pen," p. 32).

If the ink flows too fast, you may simply have overloaded the nib, in which case you can make some more pulling strokes on the spare piece of paper until the flow is correct. Alternatively, the reservoir may be fitted too close to the edge of the nib, or a new nib may not have been properly cleared of lacquer (see p. 32). Sometimes an incompatible paper or ink is the cause (see p. 36).

Try a few strokes using a Mitchell's No. 0 nib, as shown on the facing page, to get the feel of the nib. Keep the nib in complete contact with the paper to avoid writing with ragged edges. Do not press too hard or you may force the nib apart and distort the thickness of the stroke. If pressure is too light, strokes may be hesitant, slightly ragged, or waisted.

PEN ANGLES AND PATTERNS

You are now ready to practice holding the pen at a constant angle to achieve thick and thin strokes. Try the exercises illustrated on the following pages to develop your skills in producing consistent strokes at accurate angles.

1 *Use a protractor to help you establish the pen angles on your practice sheet.*
2 *Copy the strokes shown, checking your writing against the examples and making any necessary corrections.*

SPARSE INK FLOW
You may not be pressing hard enough. Check that the reservoir's fit is not too tight and that it is not too far from the edge of the nib.

OVERHEAVY INK FLOW
The nib may be overloaded, or the reservoir may be too close to the end of the nib. Check also that no lacquer is left on the nib.

CORRECT INK FLOW
The pen is working well and produces a dense, sharp-edged stroke.

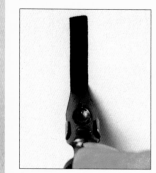

Correct   Incorrect

A clean-edged stroke depends on both edges of the nib being in contact with the paper. A ragged edge along one side of the stroke may indicate that the nib has not been aligned correctly on the paper.

FIRST STROKES

1 *Rule lines ¹/₂" (1 cm) apart, and practice downward vertical strokes with a Mitchell's No. 0 nib held horizontally (0°) to the writing line.*

2 *Keeping the nib at 0° try writing some horizontal strokes between your writing lines from left to right.*

3 *Make further horizontal strokes, but now practice pushing them up and then pulling down at the ends.*

PRACTICING HEIGHT AND SPACING

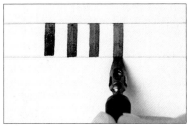

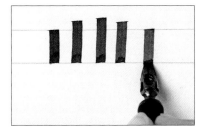

1 *With lines ruled as before, practice parallel downstrokes. Concentrate on making them the exact height of the writing lines.*

2 *Starting with a stroke at the height of the writing lines, draw parallel strokes progressively taller, then progressively smaller, as shown.*

3 *Repeat stage 2, but this time concentrate on spacing the strokes as evenly as possible.*

PRACTICING PEN ANGLES

0° *Establish the angle.*

0° *Downward vertical pull.*

0° *Left-to-right horizontal.*

0° *Vertical and horizontal.*

30° *Establish the angle.*

30° *Downward vertical.*

30° *Left-to-right horizontal.*

30° *Combined vertical and horizontal.*

PRACTICING PEN ANGLES (continued)

45° *Establish the angle.*

45° *Downward vertical.*

45° *Left-to-right horizontal.*

45° *Vertical and horizontal.*

90° *Establish the angle.*

90° *Downward vertical.*

90° *Left-to-right horizontal.*

90° *Vertical and horizontal.*

MULTIPLE STROKE PRACTICE
Vertical strokes

Practice parallel vertical strokes between your writing lines at pen angles of 30° and 45° as shown at right. Try to keep the strokes evenly spaced, approximately 1 nib width apart.

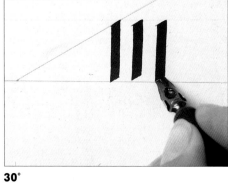

30°

45°

Horizontal strokes

Next, try some parallel horizontal strokes at 30° and 45° pen angles as shown at right. The strokes should be evenly spaced approximately 1 nib width apart.

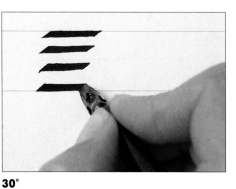

30°

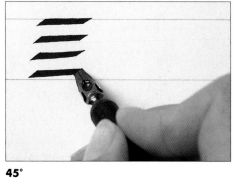

45°

Left-to-right diagonals

Now practice parallel diagonals between your writing lines at 30° and 45°. As before, try to ensure even spacing based on 1 nib width.

30°

45°

Right-to-left diagonals

Note how diagonals drawn from right to left produce a much thinner stroke. Practice these with a pen angle of 30° and then 45°. Concentrate on achieving parallel strokes at consistent angles.

30°

45°

PRACTICING CURVED STROKES

30° – Counterclockwise curve
Practice arcs based on half an O as shown.

30° – Clockwise curve
Next practice arcs in the opposite direction.

Circular O form
Now use both strokes to complete an O.

45° – Counterclockwise curve
Practice arcs based on half an oval O as shown.

45° – Clockwise curve
Next practice arcs in the opposite direction.

Oval O form
Now use both strokes to complete an O.

43

Margins

When you use your writing for a finished piece of work, the margins you choose make an important contribution to the overall effect. To show your writing to best advantage, you need to balance the text against the space around and within it. The amount of space between the lines, between areas of text, and between heading and text helps determine the proportions of the outer margins. Too much space weakens a design; insufficient space makes it look cramped. Generous margins are generally preferable to narrow ones, because surrounding space gives the text unity.

Many designs use the traditionally proportioned margins found in printing and picture framing, and these are easy to calculate (see facing page). Others may flout convention to achieve a particular effect. Each piece of work has its own requirements. Your ability to assess margins will gradually become intuitive.

Side margins should be equal, but the bottom margin should be larger than the top, so that the work does not appear to be slipping off the page. If a title or author's name is used, this should be considered as part of the text area when measuring margins.

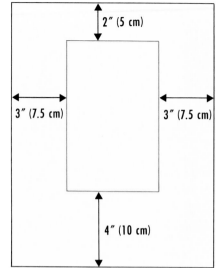

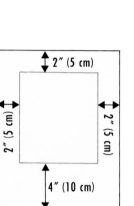

CALCULATING MARGINS: VERTICAL LAYOUT

For a vertical panel of text, the top margin is gauged by eye and doubled for the bottom margin. A measurement between these two is used for the sides. In the example above the top might be 2" (5 cm), the bottom 4" (10 cm), and the sides 3" (7.5 cm). An equal measurement for top and sides with a deeper bottom margin is sometimes appropriate (left).

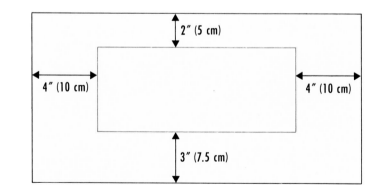

CALCULATING MARGINS: HORIZONTAL LAYOUT

For a horizontal panel of text, the widest space needs to be at the sides. In the example above the measurements are 2" (5 cm) at the top, 4" (10 cm) for the sides, and 3" (7.5 cm) for the bottom margin. An alternative formula is shown at left. Side margins should be equal.

Cardboard strips can be used as a framing device to help you determine the most suitable margins for your work. Make a collection of strips in varying sizes from 2–4" (5–10 cm) wide: four of each width at different lengths (two long, two short). L-shaped pieces of cardboard or matboard can also be used. You may be able to obtain scraps from a picture framer, or you could use old mats cut into L-shapes that will together form an adjustable rectangle.

1 Place the strips, or L-shaped mats, like a frame.

2 Here the text is "lost" within overly wide margins. Experiment by moving the strips toward and away from the edges of the text.

3 Take care not to cramp the text between narrow side margins, as occurs here.

4 When the balance between text and white space looks right, mark the chosen margins with a light pencil point in each corner.

The hours when the mind is absorbed by beauty are the only hours when we really live, so that the longer we can stay among these things, so much the more is snatched from inevitable time

HORIZONTAL LAYOUT
In this piece (above), the space on either side of the text is filled with pale flourishes, which extend the width of the layout. The bottom margin is slightly greater than the top one, thereby "supporting" the text.

VERTICAL LAYOUT
This panel of poetry (left) achieves visually equal margins at the top and sides by measuring the top margin from the tops of the flourished ascenders and the side margins from their narrowest point.

45

Ruling writing lines

Ruling your own lines for writing will give you more precise results than guide sheets with preruled lines placed under your paper. It will also provide useful practice in judging letter heights and vertical spacing. Draw the lines lightly, using a well-sharpened pencil and a metal ruler or T-square.

There are several ways to rule guidelines for writing with the broad pen, and each person usually has a preferred method. None of these is complicated, but, whatever method you choose, it is important to be accurate.

The key factor is the x height (see "Letter height," p. 24). This is measured in terms of nib widths so as to ensure that letter proportions remain correct for the size of nib being used. The measurement is made by marking the nib widths in a series of small blocks that form a "staircase" or "ladder" of the required height (see above right). Therefore if you are using a script written with an x height of 4 nib widths, you will build a "staircase" of four blocks to represent the height of the writing line. It is helpful to use dividers to "hold" the measurement of the x height for transfer to your writing sheet. Alternatively, you can mark it in pencil on a strip of paper.

The spacing between writing lines, called interline or just line spacing, is a multiple of the x height (see p. 21). Take it from your first set of nib width measurements and hold it with a second pair of dividers or add it to your strip of paper. Transfer the letter height and line spacing measurements to your writing sheet by means of small penciled lines — marked down both sides of the sheet to ensure accuracy. You can then rule your lines from these marks, using a ruler and triangle aligned with the edge of the paper (see p. 21).

MEASURING BY NIB WIDTH

Write the nib width blocks by holding the nib vertically and pulling it briefly to the right (or to the left, if you are left-handed). You can create a vertical "ladder" (right) or a "staircase" (far right).

USING DIVIDERS

1 *Set the dividers to the height of your "staircase" of nib widths.*

2 *Place the dividers on a previously marked guideline indicating the top of your first line, and mark the baseline at each margin. Rule the baseline.*

USING A T-SQUARE

A large T-square of the type shown can assist in the ruling of guidelines. Because it enables you to draw parallel lines, you need only mark the line depths along one margin.

Ruling your writing sheet

The method of measuring writing lines in nib widths is the best way to ensure accurate letter proportions. You can save time by making a collection of marker strips for different scripts and nib sizes to reuse when ruling writing lines in the future.

1 *Line up a strip of paper with the top edge and left margin of your paper, and mark the position of the top of the x height on both the paper and strip.*

2 *Mark the right margin in the same way, using the same marked paper strip as a guide.*

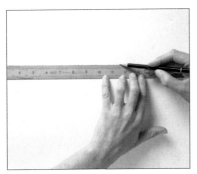

3 *Rule a line between the two margins.*

4 *Use your chosen nib to create a "staircase" or "ladder" guide for the x height — in this case 3 nib widths — on a piece of scrap paper.*

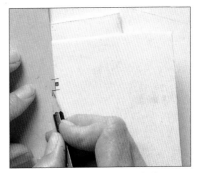

5 *Place the paper strip used above against the ladder, aligning the marked point with the top. Mark the base of the x height on the strip.*

6 *Place the strip on the paper with the top mark aligned with the line you previously ruled. Mark the baseline on the left and right margins, and rule a line across.*

7 *Mark the interline space on the strip beneath the x height guide. Measure multiples of the x height you have already marked.*

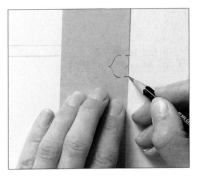

8 *Using the interline space mark on your paper strip, mark the top of the x height for the next line on both margins and rule this on the paper. Continue marking the x height and the interline spaces for the required number of lines.*

47

Layout basics

Layout is the arrange-ment of text (and any illustration) on the page. The aim is to bring to-gether the visual and tex-tual content of the work in a way that is attractive, harmonious, and legible. To some extent layout will be dictated by the purpose of the work, the degree of formality or freedom involved, and the mood that is sought. No single format will suit every case. Creative decisions always depend upon individual judgment. This is an exciting area for discovery, but there are for-mulas and guidelines to help you.

Layouts can have a vertical or horizontal shape, and text may be aligned left, aligned right, justified, centered, or asymmetrical (see facing page). Deciding which arrangement to choose means considering the overall texture of a piece of work in terms of positive and negative shapes — marks on the page and the spaces between them. Accustom your eye to looking for weak features when planning your layout, and aim for positive rather than under-stated contrasts, such as large and small, dark and light, strong and weak.

The choice of layout also depends on the sense and mood of the text, and the way it divides into lines. For a poem, line endings need to be kept as the poet wrote them. In interpreting prose, line breaks can be planned to enhance the meaning of the text. It is usual to have lines of five to nine words in a relatively lengthy text. In short texts just one or two words per line can provide an interesting layout. Line spacing and the style of script — tall or laterally spreading letters — will also affect the shape of the text area. It is useful to begin by making thumbnail sketches — small, quickly delineated inspirational drawings that play with design ideas.

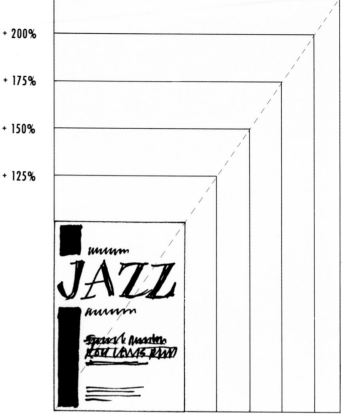

+ 200%

+ 175%

+ 150%

+ 125%

SIZING UP

To convert your thumbnail sketches to full-size layouts, draw a diagonal line from the bottom left corner of the thumbnail to the top right of the larger sheet, as shown in the diagram. If the measurement is twice the size of the original, for example, all measurements should double, including the nib size. An alternative method is to use a photocopying machine that records the percentage of enlargement.

Factors that affect your choice of layout:
- ✔ *Who is the text for?*
- ✔ *Where will the text be displayed?*
- ✔ *How much text is there?*
- ✔ *Are there other components — heading, subheading, author, title, or date, for example?*
- ✔ *Is the text poetry that must retain its line scheme?*
- ✔ *Is the text prose, and where should line breaks come?*
- ✔ *How long are the lines?*
- ✔ *What is the meaning of the text?*
- ✔ *What is the mood of the text — lively, static, formal or informal, for example?*
- ✔ *Does the text need decoration, and of what kind?*

TYPES OF LAYOUT

CENTERED

The writing lines are balanced equally on either side of a central line (drawn faintly in pencil for guidance and erased when writing is complete). This symmetrical layout is often useful when balancing long and short lines. A centered layout is most suitable for poetry or short prose pieces.

ALIGNED LEFT

All writing lines begin from a straight vertical left margin. This gives a strong left edge and a softer right-hand effect. Avoid marked variations in line length and split words. This is a versatile layout, used for both poetry and prose.

ALIGNED RIGHT

The lines are aligned vertically on the right. This layout can be effective in giving tension to a design in a slightly unexpected way. But it takes practice to achieve the necessary accuracy of letter widths and spacing. This layout is often seen in short texts such as letterheads.

ASYMMETRICAL

This is a layout that does not conform to an established alignment and yet maintains a sense of balance. A key feature is the nonalignment of most or all line beginnings and endings. The informality of the layout lends itself to texts of all kinds where this effect is appropriate.

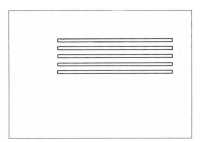

JUSTIFIED

Both right and left edges are vertically straight. Skill is needed to calculate word spacing to achieve this effect. Justified layouts produce a formal effect that is useful for prose work.

49

Cutting and pasting

THE BASICS OF BROAD-PEN CALLIGRAPHY

Planning a layout and making a draft version to guide your final work is best done by the method known as "cut and paste." This avoids the process of repeatedly rewriting a text in a particular format each time a problem arises. Cutting and pasting enables you to reassemble the text quickly and accurately in numerous alternative layouts. It allows you to "play" with the text and in that way discover a range of approaches.

Begin by writing your text on layout paper. Cut this into lines or words, and place them on a clean sheet of paper large enough to allow the text to be moved around and with adequate surrounding space for the calculation of margins (see p. 44). Move the strips around freely to evaluate different arrangements. It is a good idea to write the text twice so that you can try alternative layouts with the same wording and compare them side by side.

When you have finalized your decisions about overall shape, line length, and spacing, rule writing lines at the chosen height and paste the text in place. You now have a rough pasteup from which to copy your finished work. A step-by-step demonstration of the cut-and-paste method is shown on the facing page.

To center text during the cut-and-paste stage of layout planning (see p. 48), fold each cut line of writing in half, so that the first and last letters cover each other. Then align this center fold with the vertical line at the center of your page and paste it down. When writing the final version, take careful measurements from the centered draft layout, marking each line beginning and ending with a penciled dot. Alternatively, use a photocopy of the centered layout text, cut and fold it line by line, and keep it directly above your work for reference while you write the text in its final version.

CUTTING AND PASTING EQUIPMENT
For cutting and pasting you will need a craft knife and glue. Rubber cement that allows you to reposition the text until you are happy with the result is the best glue for this purpose.

ASSESSING YOUR LAYOUTS

Having cut and pasted your text into a provisional layout, you need to be able to make a judgment on its merits. Train your eye to look for balance and variety in the distribution of text within your chosen margins. The illustrations in this box show examples of the types of faults you should be on the look out for in your own pasteups.

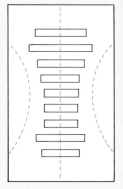

Top heavy layout

Third line too long, leaving insufficient left margin

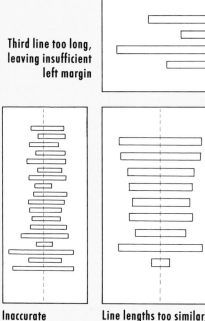

Inaccurate centering

Line lengths too similar, bottom line too short

Insufficient bottom margin

Cutting and pasting a layout

The materials needed for cutting and pasting are a sheet of layout or drawing paper measuring at least 11" × 17", scissors, a ruler, and glue such as rubber cement, that allows you to reposition pieces of text.

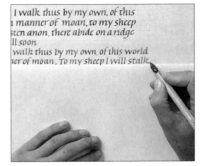

1 Write your text in the chosen script and size. This is italic script, written at an x height of 4 nib widths.

2 When the ink is dry, cut the writing into lines using scissors or a craft knife and metal ruler.

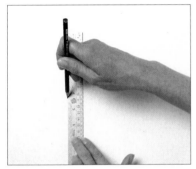

3 Rule a vertical line in pencil on a sheet of layout paper, approximately 2" (5 cm) from the left edge.

4 Assemble the strips of writing on the sheet, beginning against the penciled line. Move the lines to various positions across the sheet to observe the effect on shape.

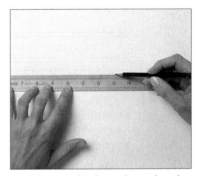

5 After you decide on the preferred layout, mark and rule the lines on the layout paper.

6 Apply rubber cement along the writing lines.

7 Position the strips of text and press them into place. Repositioning is possible if necessary.

8 When the rubber cement is dry, rub away any excess with your fingers to leave a neat and securely glued rough pasteup.

Broad-nibbed pen principles

The edged-pen, or broad-nibbed pen, builds up a letterform stroke by stroke, in the way you have practiced in pencil (see "A basic alphabet," p. 22). But a pen-made letter is composed of thin and thick strokes made by keeping the nib edge at a constant angle to the writing line. The width of the stroke varies according to the direction in which you move the pen while maintaining that fixed nib angle. Pen angles are specific to each script and an essential part of its individuality. A script written with a pen angle of 45°, for example, will look different from one formed mainly at 30°. Some scripts use a single pen angle and others call for changes.

KEY CHARACTERISTICS

Pen angle is not the only feature that helps define a script. Listed opposite are eight characteristics that define and distinguish all the scripts in this book. At the start of each script you will find a panel that profiles the script in terms of these characteristics.

HEIGHT AND WEIGHT

Letter height is measured in nib widths of the chosen nib size (see "Ruling writing lines," p. 46). The size of the nib and number of nib widths determine the density, or weight, of the script. There are recommended letter heights for each script based on historical examples. It is advisable to gain experience with these before exploring alternatives.

PEN ANGLE

The broad-nibbed pen is held at a constant angle to achieve thick and thin lines. A recommended pen angle for each script, based on historical precedent, gives the correct distribution of weight to the letters. It may be helpful in the beginning to measure and draw the main angle of a script with a protractor (see "Making a mark," p. 40).

SLANT

All the thick downstrokes of a script, except diagonals, must slant consistently at the correct angle for that script, or letters will appear unmatched. Writing with a consistent slant is achieved by matching each successive downstroke to its predecessor and requires practice. The correct pen angle and the correct slant must be maintained simultaneously.

abcdefghijklmn
opqrstuvwxyz
ABCDEFGHIJKLMNOPQRSTUVWXYZ

ITALIC SCRIPT – Gareth Colgan

ROMAN CAPITALS — Liz Burch

SERIF FORMS

Serifs are small introductory or finishing strokes made during the construction of a letter. Their shape can vary but must harmonize with the script. They are sometimes termed "roof and root" lines because of the repeating pattern they create along the top and bottom edges of the writing line. This pattern determines the uniformity of letters within the word shape.

O FORM

In many scripts o is the key letter shape because the formation of the other letters is related to it. For example, in the basic script, the arch structure of m, n, and h and the curved parts of letters such as a, b, c, and d show the roundness of the fully circular o. The same rounded shape is used for serifs. In contrast, italic is based on an oval o.

STROKE ORDER AND DIRECTION

This is the sequence in which you write the component strokes of a letter and the direction in which the pen travels, being either pulled or pushed. It is important to follow the stroke sequence, which has evolved as a natural consequence of writing from left to right and gives optimum spacing, rhythm, and flow to emerging letters.

ARCH SHAPE AND STRUCTURE

One of the main features of a lowercase, or minuscule, script is the arch structure in letters such as m, n, and h. The arch shape often reflects the form of the key letter o, and stroke direction and sequence are vital to accurate arch formation. The details of arch structure are explained along with the relevant scripts.

SPEED

Certain scripts, such as the basic script, are written slowly with many pen lifts and few push strokes, giving a characteristic formality and elegance. Others, such as italic, are written at greater speed with the pen being pushed, pulled, and rarely leaving the paper, which produces a rhythmic, flowing quality. You will need to write most scripts slowly at first to get used to forming the letterforms accurately, but you will develop the right speed with practice.

53

Basic broad-pen script

The Arts and Crafts Movement of the late 19th century and early 20th century generated a revival of interest in illuminated manuscripts and in formal calligraphy. At this time inspiration was drawn from the 10th-century Ramsey psalter, or book of psalms. Although they have numerous contemporary sources from which to choose — and make their own adaptations — today's calligraphers also continue to use the models of the past. The letter heights and pen angles recommended for the broad pen are based on those that produced the balanced proportions of traditional writing.

The information and exercises that follow will help you begin. They will also enable you to put your basic script writing to creative use. The planning and production of a piece of calligraphic work offer additional practice, as well as providing experience with layout, design, and use of materials.

Pencil skeleton forms reveal the underlying structure of letters and enable you to practice stroke sequence and spacing. When you make letters with the pen, you incorporate variations of weight, or thickness. These are determined by the angle of the pen and the direction of your stroke. If your pen is at a 30° angle to the writing line, a straight stroke will only be as wide as the nib can make it at that angle. This will become obvious with practice, but it is essential to hold the pen at the required angle and to follow any changes in pen angle necessary for particular letters; otherwise the thick and thin parts of the letters will not have the correct width and may not be in exactly the right place.

PEN, BRUSH, AND INK

For your first script with the broad pen use a good quality black calligraphy ink loaded into your pen with a brush.

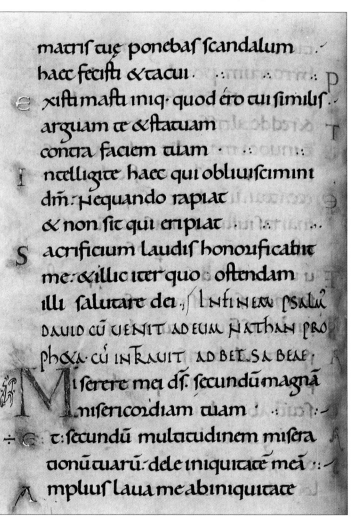

THE RAMSEY PSALTER

This text is from an English manuscript of the late 10th century. It is one of the chief sources for modern roundhand lettering.

Ausculta, o fili, praecepta magistri,
et inclina aurem cordis tui
et admonitionem pii patris libenter excipe et
efficaciter comple; ut ad eum per obedientiae
laborem redeas, a quo per inobedientiae desidiam
recesseras ▾ Ad te ergo nunc mihi sermo dirigitur,
quisquis abrenuntians propriis voluntatibus,
Domino Christo vero Regi militaturus, obedientiae
fortissima atque praeclara arma sumis ✠

THE RULE OF ST BENEDICT
Joan Pilsbury

This panel written on vellum shows the suitability of roundhand scripts for formal work. The versal initial letter and the use of two sizes of text provide added interest. The generous interline spacing contributes to the legibility of the whole. Dimensions: 8" × 5" (20.5 cm × 12.5 cm).

CHARACTERISTICS

The basic script is characterized by its rounded forms, based on a circular o, and vertical stems.

LETTER HEIGHT
4½ nib widths x height. Ascenders and descenders: 3 nib widths.

ARCH SHAPE AND STRUCTURE
Based on a segment of a circle, emerging high from the stem.

O FORM
Circular

PEN ANGLE
30° for most letters 45° for left-hand diagonals of v, w, x, y. 0° for z diagonal.

STROKE ORDER AND DIRECTION
Letters are formed with frequent pen lifts and use mainly pull strokes. These characteristics help to give this script a formal quality.

SPEED
Moderate and rhythmic.

SLANT
None, keep letters vertical.

SERIF FORMS
Not used for most basic version of this script, but may be added later. Round hooks, echoing the circular o, are the most suitable.

DOUBLE PENCILS

One way to make the transition from pencil to pen-made forms is to practice the basic letters with double pencils. The two pencil points act like the corners of the broad nib, producing the same strokes in weighted outline form. They will help you see how thick and thin strokes form naturally as a result of the angle of the writing edge on the paper and will give you a clear demonstration of letter construction. A carpenter's (chisel) pencil can also be used for your first work with weighted letters.

1 *Prepare your pencils as shown on page 30. The points should be 1/4" (6 mm) apart.*
2 *Use a single pencil to rule lines 1 1/8" (27 mm) apart.*
3 *Practice the letters shown. Hold the double pencils at 30° to the horizontal for all strokes. This is the same angle as that you will use with the broad-nibbed pen.*

BASIC PEN STROKES

The nib used in the basic script pen exercises is a Mitchell's No. 1 1/2, which is large enough to show letter details clearly.

1 *Rule lines at an x height of 4 1/2 nib widths of a Mitchell's No. 1 1/2 nib.*
2 *Following the diagram at right, practice the thick vertical downstrokes. Keep the pen angle at 30°, and try to achieve vertical strokes with sharp edges. All your strokes should be the same width. The width will vary if you change the pen angle or if your strokes are not vertical.*
3 *Repeat the exercise for diagonal, horizontal and curved strokes, changing the pen angle to 45° for the left-to-right diagonals. These will be used later to write v, w, x, and y.*

ARCHES

Arch structure is a defining feature of all lower-case scripts.

1 *Rule lines at 4 1/2 nib widths of a Mitchell's No. 1 1/2 nib.*
2 *Make a vertical downstroke.*
3 *Place your nib completely inside the vertical as you begin the arch stroke.*

4 *Move the nib uphill to the right, keeping it almost straight until it leaves the stem. Once outside the stem, move the nib horizontally to the right, then around and down to form a circular arch with a hint of squaring at the right side where the arch and downstroke join. Make sure that your arches follow the arc of a circle.*
5 *Practice the letters n and m until you are satisfied with the result.*

LETTER FORMATION GROUPS

Begin practicing weighted letters in their formation groups, so that you get used to the movements needed to make related strokes. These groups relate to the geometric forms described on page 23.

1 *Leave two lines blank between each writing line.*
2 *Practice each group several times, following the model closely. The arrows indicate stroke order and direction. Use a 30° pen angle for all strokes except the thick diagonals of v, w, x, y (45°), and the z diagonal (0°).*
3 *Check your letters against the model after each attempt. Make sure that the letters within each group relate, exhibiting the details common to the group.*

SPACING

The principle of even spacing is the same for weighted as for skeleton basic letters (p. 25). However, if you compare skeleton letters and weighted letters of the same height, you will notice that the weighted letters are spaced slightly closer. This is because weighted strokes take up some of the counter space (enclosed space) within letters.

1 *Rule lines at an x height of 4½ nib widths of a Mitchell's No. 1½ nib.*
2 *Write a basic script h.*
3 *Place an i next to it, slightly closer than the width of the h counter.*
4 *Place an o slightly closer to the i.*
5 *Write a c alongside the o, even closer but not touching.*

Slightly flattened curve

Softened front of bowl

Crossbar on x height

a b c d e f

Arches based on o form

Top counter circular, lower counter oval

g h i j k l m n

Right angle at join

Arch based on o form

o p q r s t u

Slightly flattened curve

Aligned vertically at right of letter

Slightly squared-off join

v w x y z

0° pen angle for diagonal

Vertical v elements

Straight right-hand diagonal

Once you are familiar with the letter groups and spacing, you are ready to write the basic letters in alphabetical order on paper ruled at an x height of $4\frac{1}{2}$ nib widths of a Mitchell's No. $1\frac{1}{2}$ nib. Write the alphabet in sections: a–f, g–n, o–u, v–z. Repeat each section several times, checking pen angle, letter shapes, and spacing each time before rewriting. Use the Rule of Three (p. 25) to help you verify spacing.

CHECKLIST

✓ Keep your letters vertical.

✓ Keep your pen at an angle of 30° to the writing line, except for the thick left-hand diagonals of v, w, x, and y (45°) and the z diagonal, written with a flat pen (0°).

✓ Make sure that the bodies of your letters fill the double line (except g).

✓ Check that the arches form an arc of the circular o.

✓ Make sure that stroke joins occur at the same height in letters of the same formation group, such as h, m, n, and r or q and d.

✓ Make sure that the base curves of t, and u relate to the circular o.

✓ Check that the crossbars of t and f coincide with the top writing line. The base curve and crossbar of t should align on the right.

✓ Ensure that the two halves of m and w are equal.

✓ Keep ascenders and descenders 3 nib widths above and below the line (see "Characteristics," p. 55).

ALTERNATIVE FORMS AND AWKWARD JOINS

Some letters have alternative forms. If you choose an alternative, it is usually preferable to keep to it throughout a piece. Also shown are some letter combinations that sometimes cause difficulty, especially with spacing.

1 *Rule lines at an x height of 4¹/₂ nib widths of a Mitchell's No. 1¹/₂ nib.*
2 *Practice each of the letters shown below.*
3 *Then practice the letter combinations in the second line.*

WORD PRACTICE

Once you are able to write and space the alphabet accurately, begin writing words. Trying the letterforms in new combinations will consolidate your knowledge of their shapes and extend your experience of spacing. It is best to concentrate on writing the same few words repeatedly at first. The area between words should be consistent: leave space for a basic script o.

1 *Write at an x height of 4¹/₂ nib widths of a Mitchell's No. 1¹/₂ nib.*
2 *Leave the width of an o between words.*
3 *Warm up by writing a line of "nini," treating it as if it were a word. Straight-sided letters are written equidistantly and are therefore easier to space.*
4 *Practice each of the words shown at right several times, checking each time for accuracy of letterform, pen angle, and spacing.*
5 *Apply the Rule of Three spacing check (p. 25) to each word.*

nave

lace hall

letter

cattle

Basic script greeting card

Now that you have mastered the essentials of this basic weighted script, you can begin to use your skills in simple decorative projects such as this attractive greeting card, written with a Mitchell's No. 1½ nib and decorated with gouache applied with a pen and a brush.

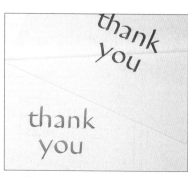

1 *Write out the words on lines ruled to 4½ nib widths. Cut and paste the lines into a centered layout (see p. 50). Copy carefully onto folded paper.*

2 *Rule margins onto the pasted-up version (see p. 44), and try out a simple border decoration in gouache. Copy the border onto your final version.*

Writing a short quotation

Planning and writing a short quotation gives you practice in rhythmic writing, spacing, and design. Use a Mitchell's No. 1½ nib. Write the final version over a watercolor wash in colors that echo the text.

1 *Write out your text on layout paper between lines ruled at 4½ nib widths. Do not worry about making decisions on layout at this stage.*

2 *Cut the text into individual words, and experiment with different layouts. When you have decided on a layout, paste the words into position. This then acts as a guide for the final version. A centered layout has been chosen here.*

3 *The next stage is to prepare the background. Apply a mixed watercolor wash with a large soft brush. (See also "Using color," p. 124.) The watercolor paper used here is heavy enough not to require stretching.*

4 *Allow several hours for the wash to dry. Dust with gum sandarac (see p. 37), and lightly rule writing lines. Write the words in dark blue gouache.*

Finished piece *The final text is an attractive piece of decorative calligraphy.*

DOWN IN SCALE

The smaller the script, the less contrast there is between thick and thin strokes. Greater precision is therefore needed when writing with small nibs. When you start to practice using small nibs, work your way gradually down the nib sizes, so that you do not lose pen control. Keep your sample letters at 4½ nib widths.

1 *Begin with the largest and practice each nib size in turn, writing the basic alphabet several times, followed by words and then a short quotation.*
2 *Correct the letterforms and spacing, rewriting as necessary.*
3 *Move down a nib size only when your writing is reasonably sound.*

No. 2½ o a b c d e

No. 3 o a b c d e

No. 3½ o a b c d e

No. 4 o a b c d e

No. 5 o a b c d e

WRITING LARGE

Large writing gives you practice in moving your whole arm and therefore encourages rhythmic writing. It is also helpful for detailed study of letterforms. Above all, it is fun and so encourages the flow of creative ideas. Plain stroke or border pens are ideal for large-scale writing. Large nibs devour ink and may need filling every letter. Ink can be diluted for the sake of economy when practicing, or diluted paint (watercolor or gouache) can be used. Direct dipping into ink or paint may cause blobby strokes, so try filling from a large brush (see "Loading the pen," p. 35). It is important to ensure that there is no ink or paint on the front of the nib, because this may prevent sharp writing. It is usual to write with the grooved side of the nib uppermost, which gives the best flow, but writing with the grooved side down often ensures sharper strokes. Try your pen both ways because results vary according to the individual pen and the consistency of the ink or paint. Make sure that no ink or paint dries in the nib after use. This could impede subsequent ink flow.

The best way to begin is to repeat a simple word, concentrating on forms and spacing. An interesting texture can be built up by such repetition and can later be used for a design. You may want to explore color changes in the pen (see "Color in the pen," p. 124).

COMBINING LARGE AND SMALL

Combining large- and small-scale writing can create effective contrast, but sizes must harmonize. The example at right consists of the main word written with a Mitchell's No. 1 nib and subsidiary text written with a No. 3 nib. The lettering is written in gouache on a Conté crayon background (see p. 88).

awakening

from winter's icy grip, the frozen earth thaws revealing its emerald cover

3

Mastering the letterforms

Roman capitals

The classic letterforms of ancient Rome have had a profound influence on letter design in the modern world. The Roman alphabet (based on the Greek) evolved over hundreds of years, but by the second century B.C. the Romans had established a fixed number of letters — and different ways of writing them.

Fine examples of Roman capitals are to be seen in monumental inscriptions carved in stone (in particular, those on Trajan's Column of A.D. 114). Regular, gracefully proportioned letters, the capitals were constructed according to geometric principles, using the square and subdivisions of it. They were painted onto the stone with a square-edged brush before being incised with a chisel. The design of the letters, with its marked contrast of thick and thin strokes, was therefore influenced by the action of an edged tool.

There were two types of broad-nibbed Roman capitals used contemporaneously with inscriptional Roman capitals.

The capitals, known as *quadrata* for their square shape, were written using a square-cut reed pen or quill. They were formal and written slowly. Although they bore similarities to stone-carved capitals, many of the strokes were written at a very flat angle and with considerable manipulation of the pen.

Writing was quicker with rustic capitals (see p. 170). Written with a steep pen angle, they were characterized by thin verticals and weighty horizontals and diagonals. Rustic became the principal Roman book hand, although square capitals were often retained for headings and initial letters. Rustics were also used in painted and carved inscriptions.

Contemporary calligraphers refer directly to the inscriptional letterforms as their guide for writing Roman capitals with the broad-nibbed pen.

THE MOST IS DONE
Angela Swann

This text, taken from The Aeneid by Virgil, exemplifies the use of Roman capitals in a formal context. The text is written in bleedproof gouache on watercolor paper. Dimensions: 29″ × 13″ (72.5 cm × 32.5 cm).

MAXIMA RES EFFECTA
VIRI·TIMOR OMNIS
ABESTO QUOD SUPEREST

THE MOST IS DONE AND FOR THE REST LET ALL YOUR FEARS LIE DEAD

from The Aeneid by Virgil · translated by William Morris

THAT I AM MORTAL AND DO CONFESS MY SPAN AND A DAY BUT WHEN I GAZE ON THE
THOUSANDFOLD CIRCLING GYRE OF STARS NO LONGER DO I WALK ON EARTH BUT RISE THE PEER
OF GOD HIMSELF TO TAKE MY FILL AT THE AMBROSIAL BANQUET OF THE UNDYING

STAR-GAZING Claire Secrett

*This attractive panel of a text by Plato shows
the interest and tension created by using formal
and free writing together. Dimensions:
26¼" × 8¼" (65.6 cm × 21.9 cm).*

CHARACTERISTICS

*The square is the basic model for Roman capitals, with rounded
letters formed as circles or partcircles within a square.*

LETTER HEIGHT
*7 nib widths. Some calligraphers
use 8 nib widths.*

O FORM
The O is a circle.

STROKE ORDER AND DIRECTION
*All vertical and diagonal strokes
are written from top to bottom.
Horizontal strokes are from
left to right.*

SPEED
Fairly slow.

SLANT
None.

PEN ANGLE
*30° for most letters.
45° for letters containing
diagonals (A, V, W, X, Y).
Exceptions are M, N, and Z. M
and N need 50°–60° for the thin
verticals and 45° for the
diagonals, with 30° for the last
stroke of M. Z needs 30° for the
horizontals and 0° (a flat pen) for
the diagonal to give adequate
weight.*

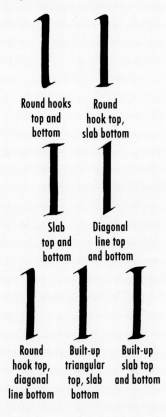

SERIFS
*Several types of serif are suitable
for the elegance of the letterforms,
including round hooks and
straight slabs.*

**Round hooks
top and
bottom**

**Round
hook top,
slab bottom**

**Slab
top and
bottom**

**Diagonal
line top
and bottom**

**Round
hook top,
diagonal
line bottom**

**Built-up
triangular
top, slab
bottom**

**Built-up
slab top
and bottom**

Skeleton letterforms

The geometric basis of Roman capitals makes a study of their skeleton forms particularly useful. Stripped to their essential form, the skeleton letters reveal the principles that govern their shapes, proportions, and the underlying relationships that unify the alphabet. A knowledge of these innate characteristics will help you identify the features needed to create well-shaped letterforms. The diagrams on the right show how Roman capitals are constructed on the basis of the square and a circle within the square. The letters are further analyzed into formation, or family, groups on the facing page.

FORMATION GROUPS

Roman capitals fall into four formation, or family, groups, based on the shared relationships shown in the geometric diagrams.

Wide circular letters: O, Q, C, G, D. The circular O provides the fundamental shape for this group. C, G, D are seven-eighths the width of the square.

Extra-wide letters: M, W. The M is based on a symmetrical V with its verticals slightly angled to fit exactly inside the base of the square. The base width of M equals its height. W consists of two adjacent V's.

Three-quarters width rectangular letters: H, A, V, N, T, U, X, Y, Z. These are based on a rectangle that is three-quarters the width of the original square.

Half-width letters: B, P, R, S, K, E, F, L. These are based on two small circles within squares, half the width and approximately half the height of the basic full-size square. The top circle and square are slightly smaller than the bottom ones. If the letters were wider, the curved parts would be egg-shaped. I and J are also included here.

Wide circular letters

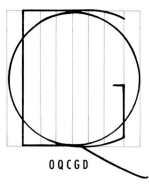

O Q C G D

Extra-wide letters

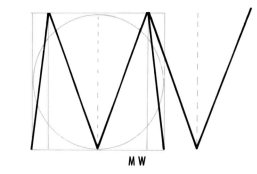

M W

Three-quarters width rectangular letters

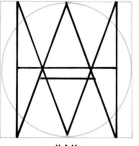

H A V

N T U X Y Z

Half-width letters

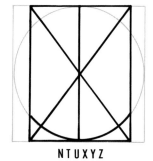

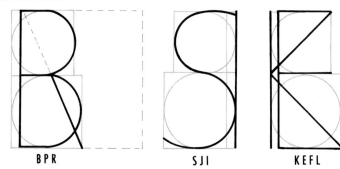

B P R

S J I

K E F L

SKELETON PRACTICE

Practice the capitals first in pencil, in their formation groups. This will give you a feel for the width of the letters. Learning the shapes and proportions, and the way in which they relate to the circular O, will prevent some of the most common mistakes that occur in pen-written Roman capitals.

1 *Rule lines ³/₄" (2 cm) apart.*
2 *Write the letters in group order, as shown below, using an HB pencil. Follow the stroke sequence indicated.*
3 *Space the letters according to the Rule of Three (see p. 25).*

SPACING AND WORD PRACTICE

This selection of words gives you practice with spacing and awkward letter combinations. Always ensure an equal area between letters.

1 *Write the words shown at right in pencil between lines ruled at ³/₄" (2 cm).*
2 *Tricky combinations are TT and LL, which should not be too far apart, or adjacent diagonals, such as AV, which should not be spaced too closely.*
3 *Write each word several times, adhering closely to the model.*

Weighted letterforms

Before using a broad-nibbed pen to make your first attempts at weighted Roman capitals, try writing the letterforms with double pencils. The two points work like the corners of a broad nib and will reveal the principles behind pen-made forms. Full instructions for making double pencils are given on page 30. An alternative is to use a carpenter's (chisel) pencil.

FREELY-WRITTEN ROMAN CAPITALS

This informal decorative treatment is rendered in gouache with ½" (13 mm) plain-stroke and multiline pens.

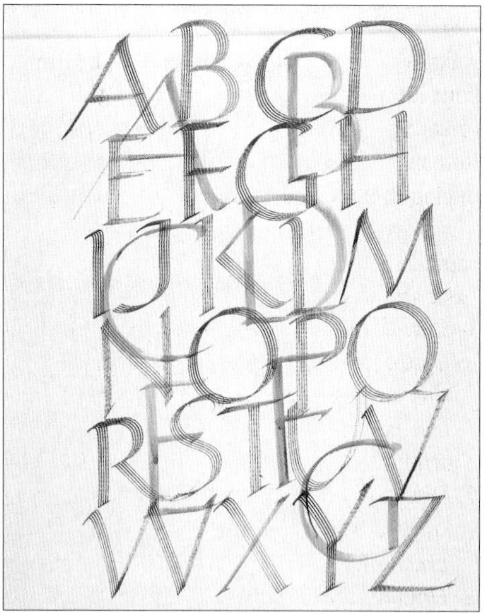

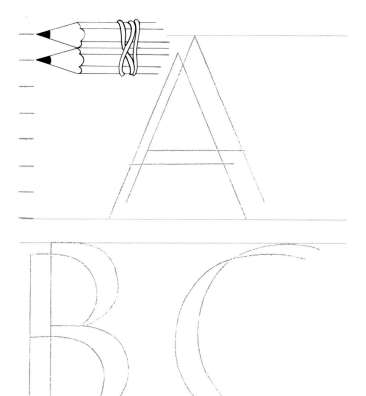

DOUBLE PENCILS

Shave the sides of two pencils with a sharp knife, so that when they are fixed together the points are about ⁵⁄₁₆" (7 mm) apart. This will enable you to write letters at the size shown.

1 *Rule lines 2³⁄₁₆" (55 mm) apart — the equivalent of 7 nib widths.*

2 *Hold the double pencils at the pen angles indicated for the different letters and write the letters shown at right.*

3 *Compare the result with the model, correct any mistakes, and then try writing the entire alphabet following the stroke order and direction indicated under "Letter formation groups," p. 66.*

STROKE PRACTICE

Before attempting complete letters with the pen, try some of the component strokes of the weighted Roman capitals (right) to make sure your nib is working properly and to get the feel of your pen. Then review the characteristics of Roman capitals and the pen angles for producing them (p. 61).

In your first practice of pen-made Roman capitals, concentrate on achieving uniform basic strokes.

1 *Rule double lines at a height of 7 nib widths of a Mitchell's No. 1½ nib. Using this large nib size for all the broad-nibbed pen exercises will enable you to see the stroke details clearly.*

2 *Dip your pen into the ink, shaking the surplus into the bottle, or load it from a brush (see p. 33).*

3 *Holding the pen at 30°, practice the vertical, the horizontal, the diagonal, and the curved strokes shown at right until you get the feel of the nib. Work to achieve sharp stroke edges.*

4 *Thick diagonal strokes and thin verticals need a steeper pen angle. Practice thick diagonals with a pen angle of 45° and thin verticals with a pen angle of 50°–60°.*

5 *Finally, practice large arcs at a 30° pen angle that relate to the O shape, and try combining them with thick vertical strokes to form a D as shown at right.*

Thick verticals – 30° pen angle

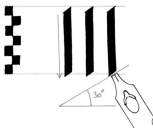

Horizontals – 30° pen angle

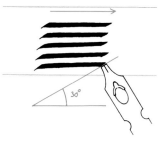

Thin diagonals – 30° pen angle

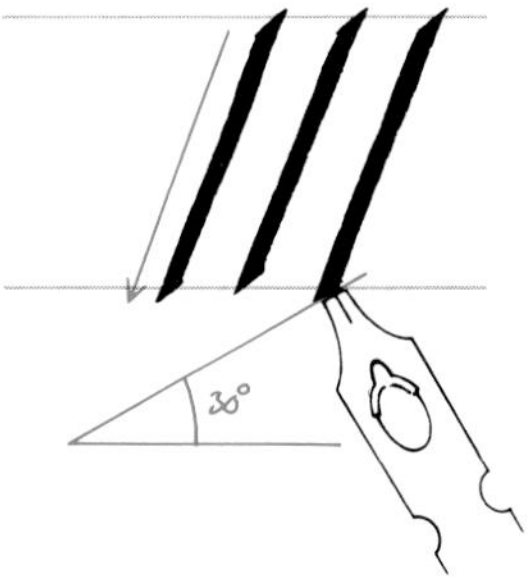

Curved strokes – 30° pen angle

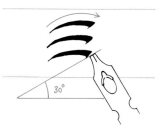

Thin verticals – 50°–60° pen angle

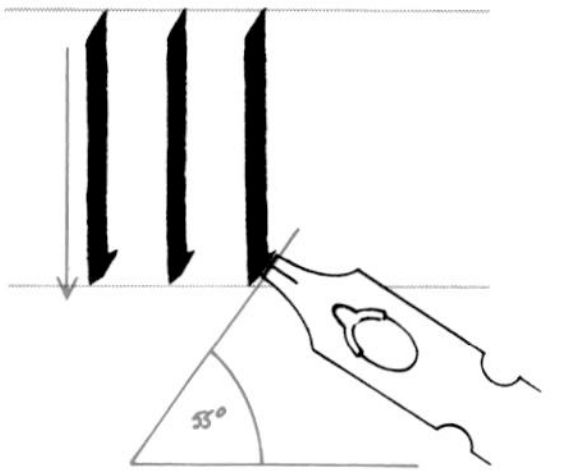

Thick diagonals – 45° pen angle

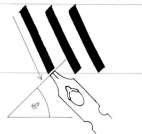

Large arcs – 30° pen angle

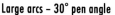

D form – 30° pen angle

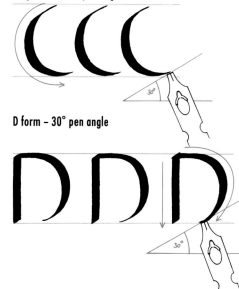

69

LETTER FORMATION GROUPS

Practice the letters in their formation groups first, because faults in width will affect spacing and be more difficult to correct later. Even if the letters look satisfactory, check them carefully against the examples. Practicing at this stage will help you avoid many common mistakes and enable you to progress more quickly.

1 Write the groups as shown below between lines ruled at 7 nib widths of a Mitchell's No. 1½ nib, leaving alternate lines blank.
2 Practice each group several times, follow the model as you write each letter. The arrows indicate stroke order and direction.
3 Check your letters against the model after each attempt. Make sure the letters are evenly spaced.
4 Refer to the watchpoints on page 72 if you need further details of letter construction.

SPACING

When spacing weighted Roman capitals, as with any script, make sure that the space inside and between letters appears equal along the writing line (see "The Rule of Three," page 25). Weighted letters should be spaced slightly closer than skeleton letters. This is because the weight of the broad nib slightly reduces the counter space (the space enclosed inside a letter) in a weighted letter compared with that in a skeleton letter of the same height. The area between weighted letters therefore has to be correspondingly smaller to maintain the balance of spacing.

Establishing the area of space between the letters in the "H I O C" diagram will help you develop accurate, even spacing when writing with a broad-nibbed pen.

1 *Rule lines to a height of 7 nib widths of a Mitchell's No. 1½ nib.*
2 *Write the H and place an I next to it slightly closer than the width of the H counter as shown.*
3 *Place an O slightly closer still, and a C even closer. Because curved letters allow slightly more space between letters at the top and bottom, they need to be placed a little closer to adjacent letters to create equal interletter space.*
4 *Rewrite the "H I O C" diagram several times (shading the area between the letters) to check that you can reproduce the same letter widths and spacing each time.*

SERIFS

Now is the time to choose the serif to match your letters. A number of serifs are suitable for use with Roman capitals, ranging from the classical to the informal. Round hooks are the simplest and a good first choice. They should be restrained and relate to the circular O. Once you have practiced these and feel comfortable writing sequences of words in weighted capitals, try using other serifs. Two variations are shown below.

Slab serifs should be straight, relatively short, and centered at the top and bottom of vertical stems. The pen angle should be no steeper than 30° or the serifs will become too chunky. A slightly flatter angle is needed for serifs on the thin strokes of A, M, and N to keep them light enough for the stem weight.

1 *Practice verticals with a round hook serif, top and bottom.*
2 *When you feel comfortable with these, practice writing other letters and words incorporating serifs.*
3 *Try the serif variations shown below on different letters.*

Round hooks top and bottom   Built-up triangular top, slab bottom   Built-up slab top and bottom

ABCDEFG

Crossbar below center | Crossbar above center | Curves joined smoothly, strokes aligned at right | Curves joined smoothly | Crossbar at center | Crossbar below center | Vertical starts below center

HIJKLMN

Crossbar above center | Curves joined smoothly | Right-angled intersection above center | Vertical and symmetrical "V" shape | Steepened pen angle for verticals

OPQRSTU

Curves joined smoothly | Crossbar at center | Crossbar at center | Aligned at right

VWXYZ

Vertical and symmetrical | Vertical and symmetrical "V" shapes | Diagonals intersect above center | Diagonals intersect at center | Horizontals align left and right

Now try the letters in alphabetical order at the same size, spacing them as evenly as possible. Use a round hook serif. Letter widths, pen angles, and spacing need to be considered simultaneously. Write the alphabet in sections: A–G, H–N, O–U, V–Z, and repeat each section several times, checking letter proportions and spacing.

CHECKLIST

✔ Check that pen angles are correct, especially for the steeper strokes of M and N.

✔ Note height of crossbars: A and F just below center. B, E, and H just above center.

✔ Join the curves smoothly in C, D, G, O, Q.

✔ Align C and G vertically at right, Z at left and right.

✔ Be sure V elements of A, M, V, W, X, Y are symmetrical and vertical.

✔ Make X and K intersect just above center, Y at center.

✔ Relate all curves to the circle.

✔ Make sure that spacing is even and adequate.

WORD PRACTICE

Begin writing words as soon as you feel confident with the alphabet, because different letter combinations put spacing to the test. Concentrate on getting a few words right before tackling a longer text. The space between words should be equal and the width of a Roman capital O.

Practice the words shown at right, which contain some tricky letter combinations. Later you can try some words of your own choosing.

1 *Write at a letter height of 7 nib widths of a Mitchell's No. 1½ nib.*

2 *Repeat each word several times, checking for letter width, correct pen angle, and spacing each time.*

3 *Apply the Rule of Three spacing check.*

NAVE

CATTLE

Writing a text in Roman capitals

Even with relatively little experience, you can interpret a simple text in a variety of interesting ways. For this Chinese saying, the text is written in white gouache on gray charcoal paper.

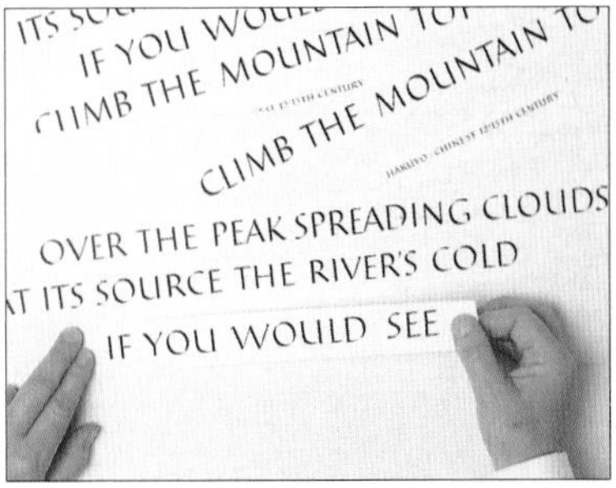

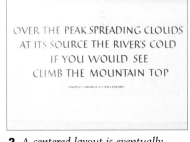

1 *The main text is written using a Mitchell's No. 1½ nib. The credit is written with a No. 4 nib. The preliminary version is photocopied and various layout options are tried by cutting and pasting.*

2 *A centered layout is eventually selected.*

3 *The final treatment is written in white gouache on gray charcoal paper on which lines have been lightly ruled.*

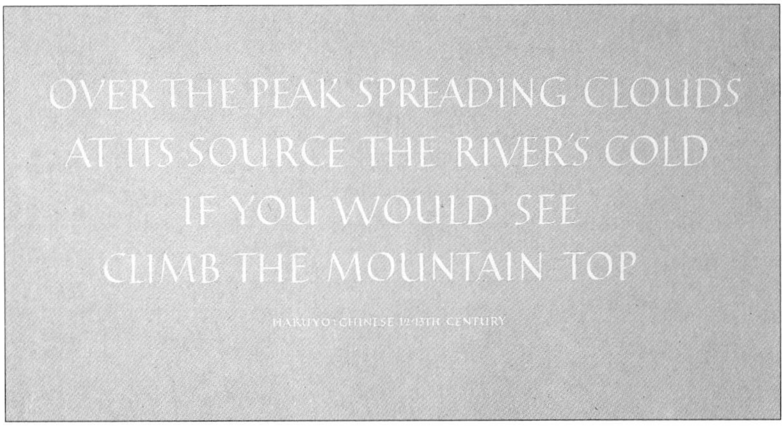

OVER THE PEAK SPREADING CLOUDS
AT ITS SOURCE THE RIVER'S COLD
IF YOU WOULD SEE
CLIMB THE MOUNTAIN TOP

HARUYO·CHINESE 12/13TH CENTURY

The finished piece *Trimmed to the required margins, the completed text makes a simple but effective statement.*

DOWN IN SCALE

So far you have been practicing Roman capitals in a fairly large nib size (Mitchell's No. 1½). Smaller nibs need greater pen control. You can learn such control by working progressively down in size. Keep to one size until you feel confident to move down. The diagram (right) shows sample letters at different nib sizes.

1 *Begin with the largest nib size shown, write the Roman capitals in their formation groups and/or in alphabetical order. Fine-tune letterforms and spacing as necessary.*
2 *The standard height of 7 nib widths is best for practice in the early stages.*
3 *Repeat this exercise in each nib size, ending with the smallest.*
4 *When writing with very small nibs, keep serifs restrained or they may weaken the letter shapes.*

No. 2   OABCDE

No. 2½   OABCDE

No. 3   OABCDE

No. 3½   OABCDE

No. 4   OABCDE

WRITING LARGE

In some ways, writing with large nibs (greater than Mitchell's No. 1½), can be as demanding as writing with small ones. Using a plain stroke pen at a height of 7 nib widths means making steady strokes over a long vertical distance. Accurate letterspacing is also more difficult because you need to stand back to see the spacing clearly. However, large pens offer exciting choices, including double and multiple stroke nibs of different widths as well as various sizes of plain stroke up to 1½" (38 mm).

When writing large, you will need to fill your pen frequently. If direct dipping into ink or paint causes blobby strokes at first, try filling from a large brush (see p. 35). Writing with the grooved side of the nib uppermost usually gives the best ink or paint flow, whereas the grooved side down usually gives sharper edges to strokes. Try your pen both ways, because results vary according to the individual pen and the consistency of the ink or paint. You may have to exert considerable pressure to write sharply with a new plain stroke pen. Make sure that no ink or paint dries in the nib after use.

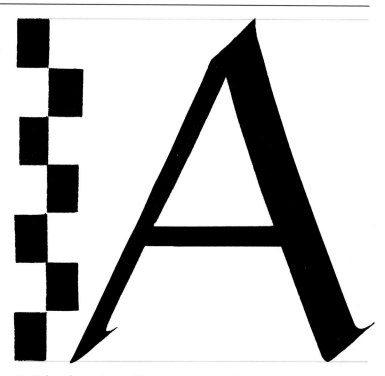

1 *Take a large sheet of layout paper and rule lines 7 nib widths apart. The Roman capital above was written at this height with a ½" (13 mm) pen.*
2 *Practice the alphabet, checking letter proportions after each attempt.*

Decorated large lettering

Roman capitals written large can be transformed by simple decorative treatments. Here, imaginative use of color and simple graphic decoration produce bold lettering that serves well as a sign or as part of a poster design. It is written with a ½″ (13 mm) pen in gouache.

1 *The first writing of the word in black ink produces some unsatisfactory letterspacing. A photocopy of the lettering is cut and pasted to adjust the spacing.*

2 *The next stage is to experiment using random letters with different color changes in the pen (see p. 124) to achieve the desired effect.*

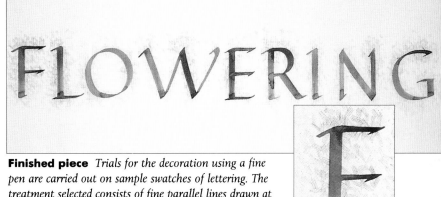

3 *The first attempt at the final lettering is started following the pasted-up model and using the selected color combination.*

Finished piece *Trials for the decoration using a fine pen are carried out on sample swatches of lettering. The treatment selected consists of fine parallel lines drawn at angles around the letters. The final version shown displays the classic qualities of Roman capitals, softened by the color selection and subtle decoration.*

VARIATION

A freer interpretation of Roman capitals encourages rhythmic writing and may be appropriate to certain texts. However, this should not be tried until you are confident of the principles behind formal Roman capitals and are able to write them accurately.

A slight forward slope, additional rhythm, and loosening of the letterforms gives greater movement to the writing. Maintain the letter proportions used for the formal capitals, and minimize the lateral compression that tends to occur when slanting the letters.

ABCDEFG
HIJKLMN
OPQRSTU
VWXYZ

Numerals

The Romans used letters to write numbers — a system that is still seen in use in certain formal contexts. In the Middle Ages, however, Roman numerals were displaced by the more versatile 10 numeric signs of the Arabic decimal system that we use today. So calligraphers "Romanized" these symbols too. Note the two versions of the number "3," both in common usage.

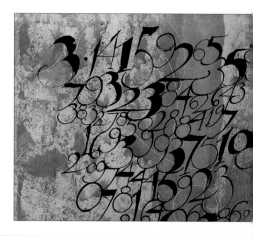

PI
John Neilson

This dynamic design shows the decorative use of numbers. The numerals are written in contrasting weights and sizes in ink .
Dimensions:
16" × 11"
(40 cm × 27.5 cm).

HEIGHT

Lined numbers are written at the same height as the capitals of the chosen script. With "old style" numerals, the 1, 2, and 0 are the x height of the script's lowercase letters; the remaining numbers descend and ascend below and above the lowercase x height and are the same height as the capitals.

SLANT AND PEN ANGLE

Numbers can be vertical and based on a circle, or compressed and slanting. However, the numeral 0 is always slightly compressed to distinguish it from a letter O. Compressed numerals suit a script of similar style, such as italic, but vertical numbers can also be used with slanting letters. Vertical numbers are written with a pen angle of approximately 30°, and the angle is slightly steepened for compressed numerals. Examples of various styles appear at right.

SPACING

Spacing ("1348," far right) should be generous for the wider, circle-based numbers and slightly closer for compressed numerals. Watch out for uneven or overclose spacing, which can cause numerals to lose their elegance.

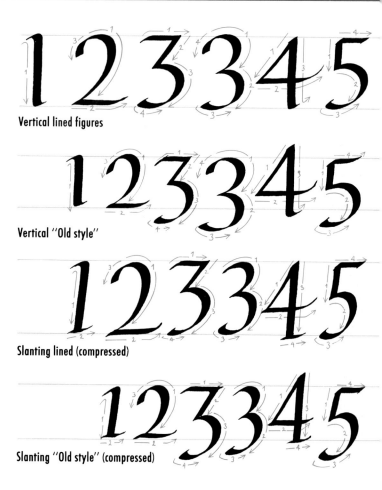

Vertical lined figures

Vertical "Old style"

Slanting lined (compressed)

Slanting "Old style" (compressed)

STYLE

Numerals in calligraphy usually match the style of the script being used. They can be either aligned at the top and bottom within the letter height ("modern" or lined) or written with some above and below the x height ("old style"). "Modern" numbers usually go with capitals for a strong effect. "Old style" numbers blend with the ascenders and descenders of a lowercase script. The examples shown at right demonstrate the different qualities of the main numeral styles used in different scripts. Note the different spacing requirements of the various examples shown.

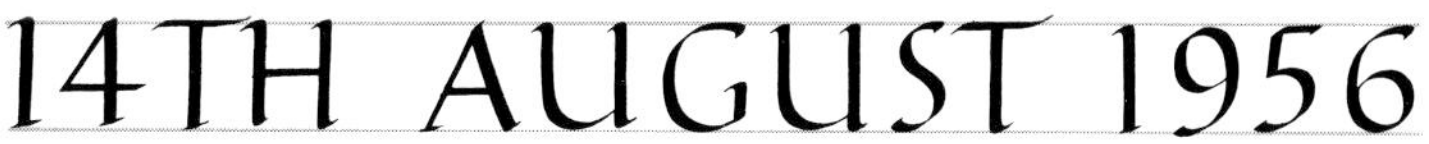

14TH AUGUST 1956
Vertical lined figures

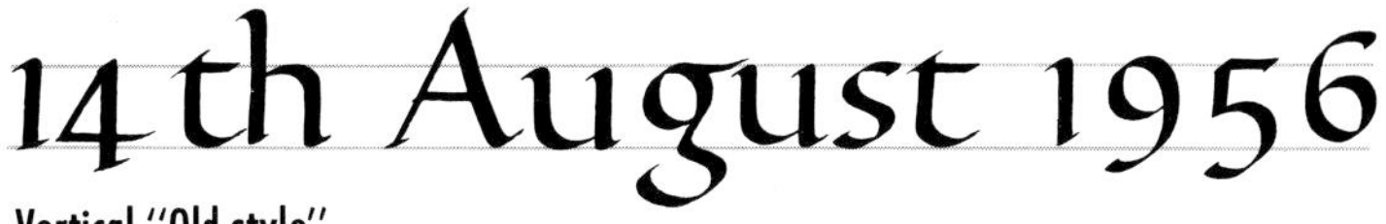

14th August 1956
Vertical "Old style"

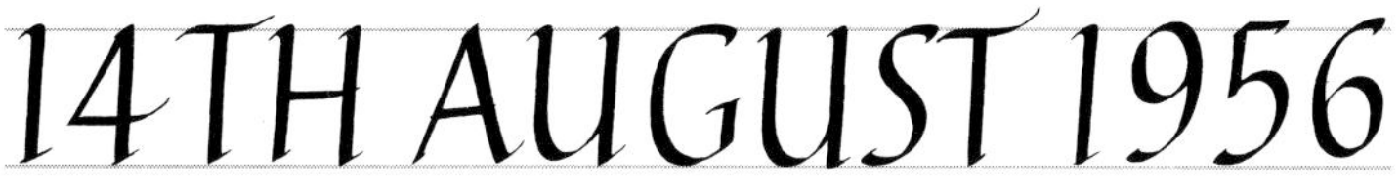

14TH AUGUST 1956
Slanting lined (compressed)

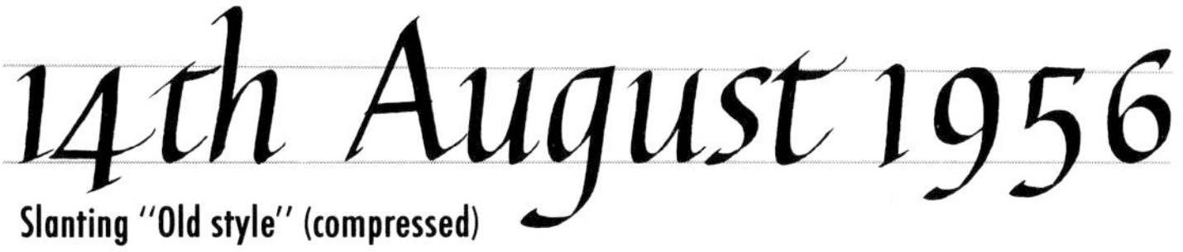

14th August 1956
Slanting "Old style" (compressed)

67890
67890
67890
67890

1348
1348
1348
1348

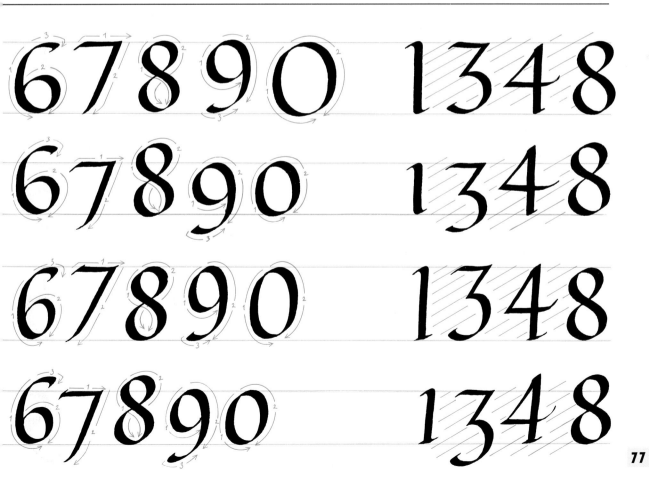

Formal italic

With its rhythmic movement and its flowing qualities, italic script epitomizes "the dance of the pen." Writing this script on a good surface can be an exhilarating experience. Italic evolved in the early 15th century and owes its name to its Italian origins. Inspired by the Carolingian minuscule scripts of ninth-century France, Renaissance scribes developed formal scripts called Humanist bookhands. Seeking a faster style to meet their increasing workload, papal scribes copying documents for the Roman chancery developed the chancery script. More quickly written than the Humanist bookhand, with narrower, forward-slanting forms, this script exhibited the flowing qualities characteristic of italic script.

In the 16th century a number of writing instruction manuals were printed from calligraphy cut on wooden blocks. The first and most famous was *La Operina* by the Venetian Ludovico Vicentino Arrighi, published in 1522. The manuals show a wealth of italics with many subtle variations. Some have few or no ligatures (connecting lines); others are emphatically cursive (joined and flowing); some have rounded letterforms; others are angular.

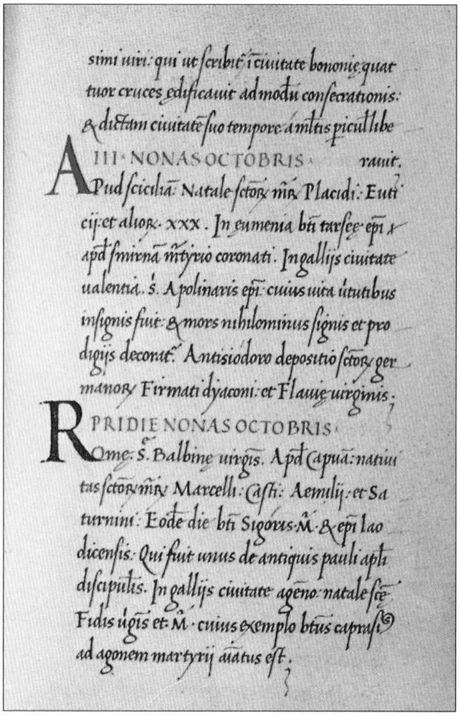

RENAISSANCE MANUSCRIPT

This fine example of Renaissance italic, with its flowing rhythm, narrow letterforms, sparing flourishes, and wide interline spacing, has an elegance that is typical of the best formal italics. The marginal capitals are a type of versal.

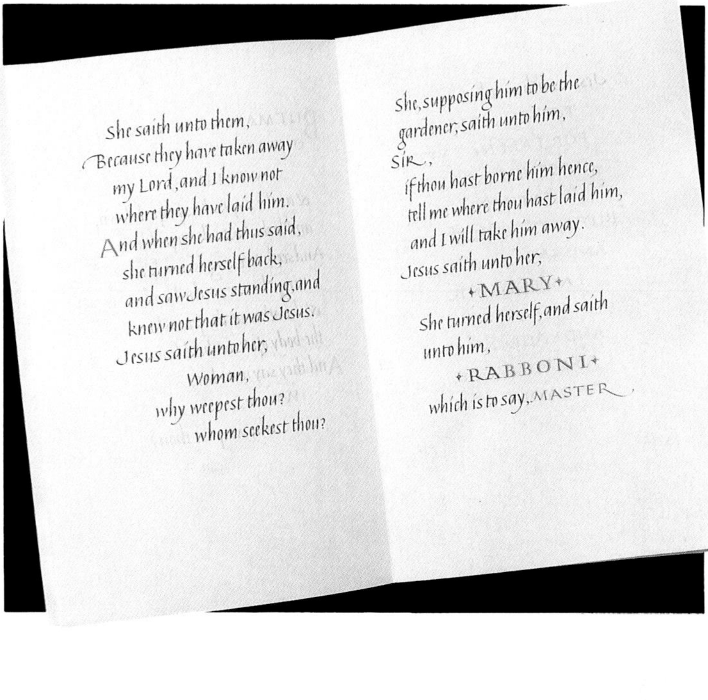

MARY MAGDALENE AT THE SEPULCHRE
Joan Pilsbury

This manuscript book written in ink on vellum shows a double-page opening in an elegant formal italic. Dimensions: 13" × 9¹/₂" (32.5 cm × 23.75 cm).

However, all exhibit the key features of the italic script: rhythmic, compressed letterforms, springing arches, forward slant, and a relatively steep pen angle of approximately 45°.

Experience with italic handwriting can help promote the fluency needed for all calligraphic work.

The contemporary calligrapher uses two basic italic scripts: formal and cursive. The formal script is an easier one for beginners. A more controlled writing method, it enables the analysis of individual letterforms, providing a sound basis from which to develop the rhythm and flow of the cursive form.

Italic is a versatile script, offering ever more opportunities as you progress. The basic formal and cursive scripts described in this book can be applied in a variety of ways and contexts, as well as providing the basis for many later experiments.

Italic is an excellent script for encouraging rhythm in writing. This is one of the key qualities of calligraphy, and it is important to develop this aspect.

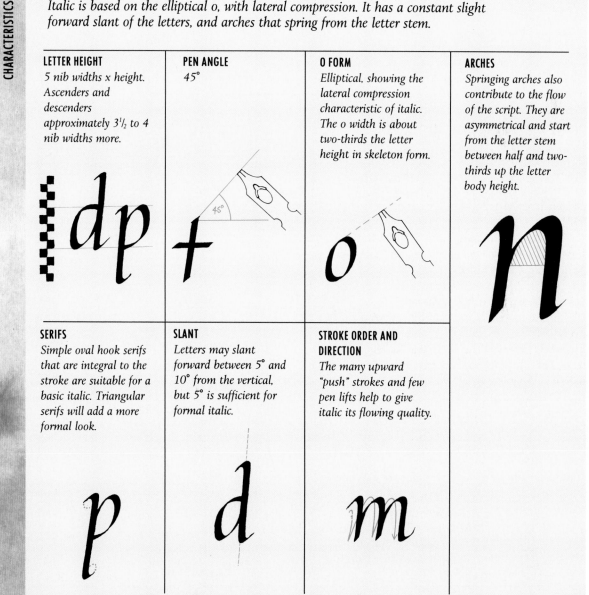

CHARACTERISTICS

Italic is based on the elliptical o, with lateral compression. It has a constant slight forward slant of the letters, and arches that spring from the letter stem.

LETTER HEIGHT
5 nib widths x height. Ascenders and descenders approximately 3$\frac{1}{2}$ to 4 nib widths more.

PEN ANGLE
45°

O FORM
Elliptical, showing the lateral compression characteristic of italic. The o width is about two-thirds the letter height in skeleton form.

ARCHES
Springing arches also contribute to the flow of the script. They are asymmetrical and start from the letter stem between half and two-thirds up the letter body height.

SERIFS
Simple oval hook serifs that are integral to the stroke are suitable for a basic italic. Triangular serifs will add a more formal look.

SLANT
Letters may slant forward between 5° and 10° from the vertical, but 5° is sufficient for formal italic.

STROKE ORDER AND DIRECTION
The many upward "push" strokes and few pen lifts help to give italic its flowing quality.

Skeleton italic

Before writing italic letters with a broad-nibbed pen, you need to learn the essential skeleton form. Remember that because italic script consists of compressed forms, all letters (except m, i, j, and w) are virtually the same width — many faults in italic are due to incorrect widths. The oval o is shown in a parallelogram with sides slanting 5° from the vertical. The o is a key to letter width though not to shape; c and e relate to o, but most italic letters relate to the arch shape.

FORMATION GROUPS

Italic letterforms are easiest to learn in groups of similar formation as shown in the geometric diagrams (right).

Clockwise arched letters: h, n, m, r, b, p, k. The group also includes i, which is the beginning stroke of the other letters. The arches spring from half to two-thirds up the x height.

Counterclockwise arched letters: l, t, u, curved y. Base curves relate to the shape of clockwise arched letters.

Diagonal letters: x, z, y, v, w. The first strokes of x, y, v, w and the third stroke of w must be relatively vertical, so that the axis of the "v" part of the letters has the same slant as the downstrokes of the script.

Oval letters: c, e, o. The c and e are the only italic letters whose shape relates directly to the elliptical o.

Triangular letters: a, d, g, q. These are softened triangles. The curve joins the straight stroke on the right side, half to two-thirds down the letter body height.

Letters with related top and/or tail curves: f, s, j. The tail curves of f and j mirror the top curve of the f.

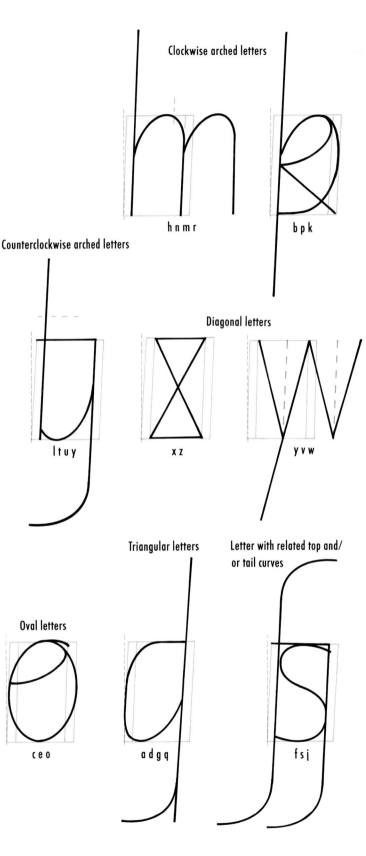

Clockwise arched letters

h n m r

b p k

Counterclockwise arched letters

l t u y

Diagonal letters

x z

y v w

Oval letters

c e o

Triangular letters

a d g q

Letter with related top and/ or tail curves

f s j

SKELETON PRACTICE

Practicing in pencil is the best way to get the feel of the script and fix the letter shapes firmly in your mind. Spending as much time as you can to acquire accurate information at this stage will make the learning of broad-nibbed italic easier and more successful.

1 *Rule lines ⁷⁄₁₆" (11 mm) apart.*

2 *With an HB pencil, write the letters in formation groups, setting out your work as shown to avoid collision of ascenders and descenders.*

3 *Follow the stroke order and direction shown in the diagrams.*

4 *Aim all straight and curved downstrokes just to the left of six o'clock to give the right amount of forward slant (about 5°).*

5 *Subtly flatten curves such as the sides of a, d, g, q; otherwise there is a risk they may become too circular.*

6 *Do not lift the pencil off the paper unless indicated by the stroke sequence.*

7 *Draw the letters lightly with the pencil until you begin to feel the form, making alterations along the way as necessary. Write each group several times before moving on to the next.*

SPACING AND WORD PRACTICE

When you feel confident with the letterforms, begin to practice writing words. To do this you will need to consider the letterspacing. Maintain equal space between all letters to achieve a balanced appearance. Try the words shown at right before attempting your own choice of words or a pencil alphabet.

1 *Rule lines ⁷⁄₁₆" (11 mm) apart.*

2 *Write the words in pencil and check the letterspacing according to the Rule of Three (p. 23).*

3 *When you are satisfied with the individual words, practice writing groups of words allowing a word space approximately the width of the o.*

Weighted italic

MASTERING THE LETTERFORMS

3

L earning a new script is exciting, and most beginning calligraphers can't wait to start writing with the broad-nibbed pen. Thorough practice of the skeleton letterforms in pencil will have familiarized you with the letterforms, stroke direction and order, and spacing considerations. But there is one more step that will help you succeed with the pen. Double-pencil italic letterforms will reveal the principle of the two overlapping skeleton shapes that produce the weighted forms. As an alternative to double pencils, you can use a chisel pencil sharpened to the width specified.

LARGE-SCALE ITALICS

Formal italics written with a broad-nibbed pen produce lively calligraphic effects.

DOUBLE PENCIL

The two pencil points represent the edge of a broad pen and are aligned at a 45° angle.

1 *Rule lines 1¼″ (32 mm) apart.*

2 *Shave the sides of the pencils so that the points are just under ¼″ (6 mm) apart.*

3 *Practice writing the letters shown at right. Follow the stroke order and direction you learned for skeleton letters.*

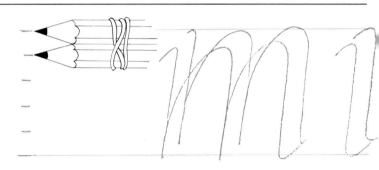

STROKE PRACTICE

As you first practice with the pen, concentrate on achieving uniform thick and thin diagonal and horizontal and vertical strokes. Practice curved strokes last.

1 *Write between lines ruled at 5 nib widths of a Mitchell's No. 2 nib, holding the nib at a constant angle of 45° for all strokes.*

2 *Make sure that the vertical strokes have a uniform slightly forward slant.*

3 *Variations in stroke width mean that you have changed the pen angle or altered the slant of the strokes.*

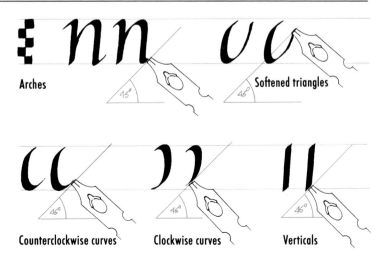

Arches

Softened triangles

Counterclockwise curves

Clockwise curves

Verticals

ARCHES

Flowing asymmetrical arches are a key characteristic of italic. Creating smooth arches with consistent shapes will help you achieve a rhythmic, even script. The springing arch leaves the letter stem between half and two-thirds up the x height, and because the nib is being pushed uphill to the right against its front edge, there is some thickness at the beginning of the springing stroke. It is important to lighten the pressure on the nib on all uphill, or push, strokes to enable the nib to move smoothly.

Practicing arches will help you acquire the rhythm and flow of italic script.

1 *Rule writing lines at 5 nib widths of a Mitchell's No. 2 nib.*
2 *Following the diagram, write a line of repeating i's, n's, and m's.*
3 *Rewrite the line, alternating the n and m with i. As these are straight-sided letters, they should be easy to space, and this will allow you to concentrate on the arches.*

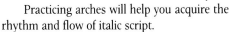

SERIFS

Oval hooks, which reflect the script's elliptical O, are a good choice for your first italic serif. In formal italic, the serifs are restrained, but a less formal, more rapidly written version will have increasingly pronounced serifs.

When you have mastered the hook serif, vary the effect by adding a sharp line serif to ascenders and descenders. To achieve a highly formal look, use a built-up triangular serif on ascenders only (see stroke order, far right), ending the descenders with a hook, sharp line, or a slightly uphill light slab.

Hook serif top and bottom

Sharp line serif top and bottom

Built-up triangular serif top, sharp line bottom

SONNET
Gareth Colgan

This passage from a sonnet by John Donne is taken from a larger work. The quill-written italics rendered in Chinese ink and watercolor on watercolor paper display rhythm and finesse. Dimensions: 24" × 11" (60 cm × 25.5 cm).

LETTER FORMATION GROUPS

Weighted letters are best learned in groups according to their shape and mode of formation. The groups are the same as for the skeleton forms.

1 *Write the groups as shown between lines ruled at an x height of 5 nib widths of a Mitchell's No. 2 nib, but leave two x heights clear between each line of writing to accommodate ascenders and descenders.*

2 *Keep the pen angle at a constant 45°.*

3 *Practice each group several times, following the model closely. The arrows indicate stroke number, order, and direction.*

SPACING BROAD-NIBBED ITALIC

Italic is an evenly spaced script and follows the Rule of Three spacing check described on page 25. You will need to practice the "h i o c" diagram with the broad-nibbed pen to get the feel of weighted spacing. Remember that curved letters are placed closer together than straight letters to create the impression of equal spacing.

1 *Write at 5 nib widths of a Mitchell's No. 2 nib, beginning with an h (use an n, if you prefer). Make sure that the letter is the correct width.*

2 *Write an i next to it, slightly closer than the width of the h counter. Place an o next to the i, fractionally closer still. Write a c alongside the o, even closer but not touching.*

3 *Rewrite the "h i o c" diagram several times.*

4 *Give yourself additional help by practicing this line: n i m i n i m i (p. 83).*

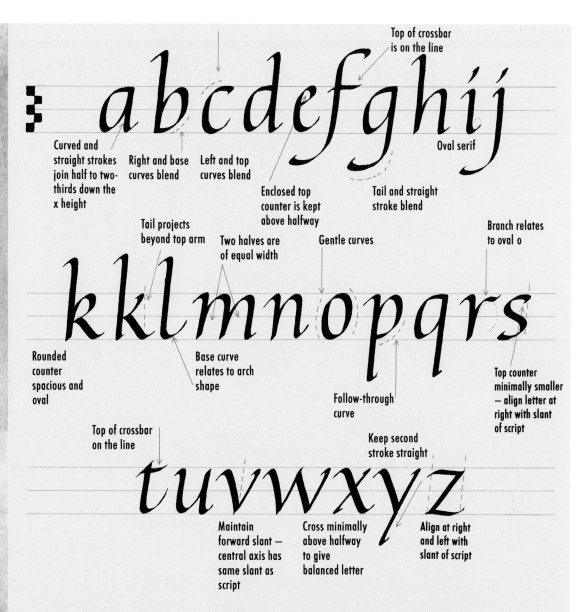

Top of crossbar is on the line

Curved and straight strokes join half to two-thirds down the x height

Right and base curves blend

Left and top curves blend

Enclosed top counter is kept above halfway

Tail and straight stroke blend

Oval serif

Tail projects beyond top arm

Two halves are of equal width

Gentle curves

Branch relates to oval o

Rounded counter spacious and oval

Base curve relates to arch shape

Follow-through curve

Top counter minimally smaller — align letter at right with slant of script

Top of crossbar on the line

Keep second stroke straight

Maintain forward slant — central axis has same slant as script

Cross minimally above halfway to give balanced letter

Align at right and left with slant of script

The italic alphabet has been labeled with important details to help you write it as accurately as possible. Look at the alphabet as a whole, and take note of these before you begin writing the alphabet.

CHECKLIST

✔ The top of the crossbars of t and f coincide with the top writing line, but can be slightly lower on f.

✔ The s and z align at the right and left with the slant of the script.

✔ The axis of v, x, and diagonally, as well as the two axes of w should have the same slant as downstrokes such as i to relate them to the slant of the rest of the script. See the v in the alphabet above as an example.

✔ All serifs are smooth, oval, and restrained.

✔ The tails of f, g, and j have smooth follow-through curves of identical shape.

✔ Check that the top and bottom curves of the o mirror each other.

✔ The curves of b and p are subtly flattened. Base curves should join the stem in a slightly downhill direction to avoid an overheavy join.

ALTERNATIVE LETTERFORMS

Letterforms may be varied where consonants combine. Double t, f, and ft may be written separately or joined by the horizontal stroke. Double f combinations may consist of two identical f's with extended descenders, joined by their horizontal bar, or a linked combination of two forms (right). Take care when writing r followed by diagonal y: the shape of the y may tempt you to overspace.

1 *Use lines ruled to 5 nib widths of a Mitchell's No. 2.*

2 *Copy the letterforms and combinations shown at right.*

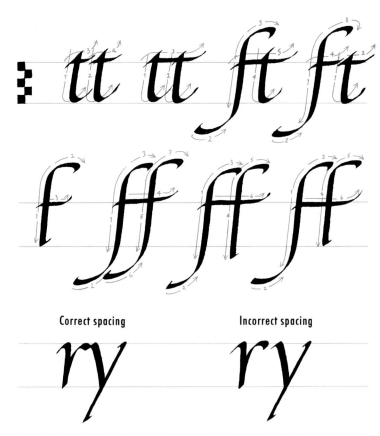

Correct spacing   Incorrect spacing

WORD PRACTICE

As soon as you feel sufficiently familiar with letterforms and spacing patterns, move on to words, which will extend your skills. Continue the practice of writing a word several times and checking the spacing and letterforms each time. Assessing your own writing gives you independence; it means you learn through understanding rather than copying. Although good writing develops gradually with practice, it requires understanding of letterform construction, which comes from adopting a critical approach from the moment you begin learning calligraphy.

1 *Write between lines ruled at 5 nib widths of a Mitchell's No. 2 nib.*

2 *Repeat each word several times, leaving room for an o between words.*

3 *Correct letters and spacing as necessary.*

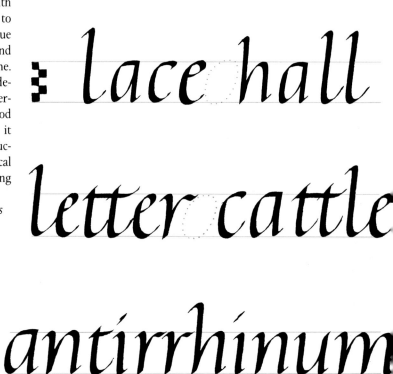

Creating texture in color

Repeated writing of the same word enables you to concentrate on letterforms, spacing, and rhythm. At the same time, you create a close-knit texture on the page, incorporating a subtle range of colors. You can use the same techniques later for exciting work with texts.

For this piece of work, the calligrapher used a Mitchell's No. 2 nib and watered-down gouache with color changes in the pen. Texture and pattern are produced by the gradated color effect and the pattern of the lettering.

1 *Write a word on alternate lines ruled at 5 nib widths of a Mitchell's No. 2 nib. At this stage decisions on the use of color and an asymmetrical layout have already been made.*

2 *A review of the first draft shows that standard spacing allows too much white space between the lines, which distracts from the textural effect desired. Your next option is to try closer line spacing.*

3 *A closer line spacing allows the ascenders and descenders to blend into the adjacent lines of text.*

4 *The final version can form part of a larger work.*

CAPITALS AND WEIGHTED ITALIC

In Renaissance times, plain Roman capitals (p. 64) were commonly used with italic. At line beginnings these were often set with a noticeable gap between capital and following italic minuscule (lowercase) letters. However, a rich variety of flourished italic capitals can also be found in Renaissance manuscripts, and the choice of capitals depends on the context and on the writer's preference. You can use Roman capitals, plain italic capitals (pp. 92–98), or flourished italic capitals (pp. 108–113) alongside italic minuscules.

Plain italic capitals are the easiest to write, although they need accurate letter-width judgment. However, the flowing lines of flourished italic capitals encourage rhythm in writing.

California,

Iowa, Ohio

Quotation in italic minuscules

Color and design are important and rewarding areas to cultivate. Designing a layout for a short text will help you blend good lettering with creative ideas.

Think about the word meanings and jot down any ideas that come to mind about color, layout, and illustration. Satisfactory layout is a matter of individual taste, but there are techniques for achieving the qualities you seek.

1 Use a 20–30 word quotation so that it can be rewritten several times if necessary without becoming too trying. Write with a Mitchell's No. 2 nib.

2 Paste up the layout using photocopies. Center the lines to avoid the square and static look of an aligned block.

3 The finished pasteup acts as a model for the final writing.

4 Try colored gouache, on a word or two. "Winter Stream" and "ice about to melt" suggest blues and purples.

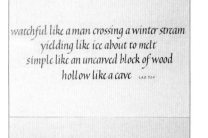

5 To give the quotation a colored background, scrape Conté colors with a craft knife and blend the powder together on the paper.

6 Gently rub the color into the paper with a tissue. Spray the background color with a fixative and dust with gum sandarac.

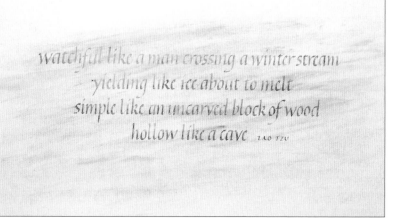

7 Add the credit to the final draft in Roman capitals using a Mitchell's No. 4 nib.

WORKING WITH LARGE PENS

Practicing any script with large pens loosens writing and encourages rhythm, because the entire arm is used and the rest of the body is more involved. It is also useful for seeing the details of letterforms, such as arch structure, and for studying any letters that seem difficult. The scale enables you to "feel" the letter more as you write, because every slight change of direction is magnified. It is also fun to play with letters and design on a large scale – allowing ideas to flow freely.

1 Write any word at 5 nib widths of a $\frac{1}{2}$" (13 mm) plain stroke pen. It's fun to experiment with different pens, but keep an eye on letter proportions, or the forms may degenerate.

2 Write in ink or one color gouache initially to get used to the pens, then try color changes in the pens.

3 When you can write the letters accurately, try working more freely and faster, creating texture on the page, or combining lowercase italic with Roman capitals.

Using large pens

Large lettering has many uses — for example, it can be used for headings and as a focal point in a panel of calligraphy. Writing large is a useful skill to master and gives you plenty of scope to be creative. With large lettering, you can let your imagination run free with innovative uses of color and layout.

1 *A variety of multi-line border pens are useful for experimentation. Here, a number of different $\frac{1}{2}$" (13 mm) nibs are tried.*

2 *The nib selected is used for the whole word with the color change in the pen (see p. 60–1). The effect is too static.*

3 *The word "dance" should really dance. Cut-up the lettering and try a layout with some vertical movement to the letters.*

4 *Move the letters until the right effect is achieved. Paste up the layout and transcribe the finished word.*

SCALING DOWN

The smaller the script, the less contrast there is between thick and thin strokes, and therefore great precision is needed when writing with small nibs. As with other scripts, a jump from large to small italic may cause you to lose control of letter shapes, so it is better to work gradually down the nib sizes.

Even if you enjoy writing small, try not to restrict yourself to any particular size, especially at first. The pronounced hand and arm movements needed for larger writing encourage the rhythm and flow that are crucial to calligraphy. Above all, don't work on too small a sheet — it may literally cramp your style. Use a sheet of at least 11″ × 17″ (29.5 cm × 42 cm) on a board of 24″ × 30″ (60 cm × 75 cm).

No. 2½   *o abcde*

No. 3   *o abcde*

No. 3½   *o abcde*

No. 4   *o abcde*

No. 5   *o abcde*

1 *Rule lines at 5 nib widths of a Mitchell's No. 2½ nib, and practice writing the alphabet several times.*
2 *Repeat this exercise in each nib size shown, ruling lines at 5 nib widths of each nib used.*
3 *Check for accuracy of shape and spacing, repeating a size if necessary before moving down. Pay close attention to stroke sharpness and letterforms, which may degenerate at the smaller sizes.*

COMBINING LARGE AND SMALL

Along with good letterforms, spacing, and rhythm, it is important to develop a sense of scale by combining different sizes of writing successfully. Combinations are generally used for contrast, but the sizes must harmonize and convey the text appropriately. Sizes should not be too similar, but there are no rules for such decisions: each text needs to be treated according to your own interpretation. A sense of what looks right in terms of text and layout develops with practice and by observing examples of well-designed calligraphy. Analyzing the decisions that have been made about scales of writing in the work of other calligraphers is invaluable for your own work.

late summer afternoon, heavy storm breaking

light mountain rain, falling veil, fading the land into oblivion

Using large and small italics

Combining large and small lettering is an effective way to add emphasis. When practicing, choose a short text so that you can maintain a good standard of writing and spacing. Read the text and decide which words you want to emphasize. In the example, the first two words are selected because they represent a complete thought.

1 Write the quote using a Mitchell's No. 4 nib. It is easier to assess where a larger nib may be needed if the whole text is written in the same nib first.

2 Paste up the small lettering using pencil marks on the edge of a separate piece of paper to judge line spacing.

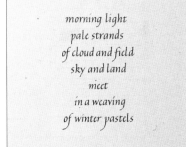

3 Complete the layout. Where line lengths vary, centering the lines is an effective way of adding movement.

4 Write the large lettering in a variety of nib sizes, from Mitchell's No. 3½ up to No. 1, on layout paper.

5 Try each size. Here No. 2 is used for the large lettering. Other good contrasts are 1½ and 3½, 2½ and 5, and 1 and 3.

6 Paste up the complete layout adding flourishes to the last line (see pp. 108–113) to give a softened effect.

7 The illustration was drawn with colored pencils, crossed by white lines made with an eraser.

Finished piece In the final work the lettering and the illustration are harmonious.

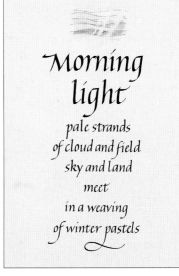

Italic capitals

The italic script was used with classical Roman capitals during the Renaissance. These were gradually modified into Humanistic square capitals and flourished italic capitals. Humanistic square capitals remained closely akin to pen-made Roman square capitals. They were often used for lines or blocks of text written entirely in capitals, as well as for line beginnings. Flourished italic capitals were a more compressed and slanting form based, like the lowercase script, on the oval O. Inventive and often exuberant, they were used for line beginnings and within italic text. Even among italic capitals, Renaissance scribes often retained the Roman capital D.

It is best to learn the compressed italic capitals without flourishes at first to establish accurate letterforms and see the relationships between the letters more clearly. Unadorned italic capitals are useful in their own right, especially for text that is to be conveyed entirely in capitals. They are suitable for formal purposes, such as presentation documents, or for the expressive interpretation of prose and poetry. You will find italic capitals versatile and flowing letterforms that offer many design opportunities.

Once you can write the plain capitals well, it is a relatively simple step to create the flourished versions described on pages 108–113.

THE PLOVER — Louise Donaldson

Written over a wash background, this calligraphic interpretation of a passage from a poem by Robert Louis Stevenson is written in three weights of italic capitals. The larger capitals are written with a plain stroke pen with color change in the pen. The lightweight letters were written with a ruling pen.

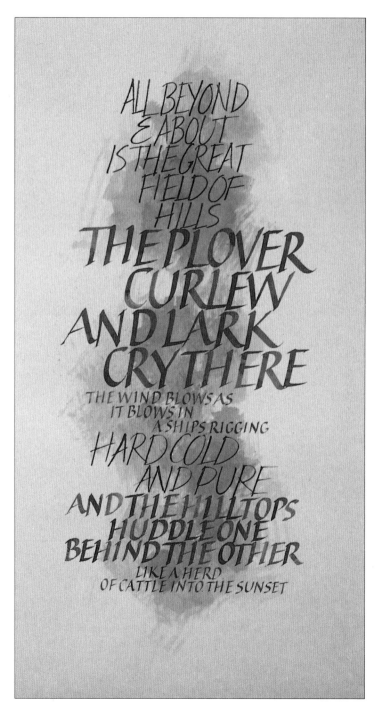

JAPANESE POEM
Liz Burch

This delicate panel (left) is rendered in large italic capitals alongside small heavyweight Roman capitals. Thoughtful placing of rubber stamp decoration creates a harmonious finished result.

PROSE PANEL
Liz Burch

This panel (right) of strong, well-spaced italic capitals demonstrates that high-quality calligraphy can make an attractive statement without the assistance of additional decoration.

THE GRAND WAY TO LEARN

IN GARDENING, AS IN
ALL THINGS ELSE
IS TO WISH TO LEARN
AND BE DETERMINED
TO FIND OUT
THE REAL WAY IS TO TRY AND
LEARN A LITTLE FROM
EVERYBODY AND EVERY PLACE

THERE IS NO ROYAL ROAD

IT IS NO USE ASKING ME
OR ANYONE ELSE HOW TO DIG-
I MEAN SITTING INDOORS
& ASKING IT. BETTER
GO AND WATCH A MAN DIGGING
AND THEN TAKE A SPADE
AND TRY TO DO IT
AND GO ON TRYING TILL IT COMES
AND YOU GAIN THE KNACK
THAT IS TO BE LEARNT
WITH ALL TOOLS OF
DOUBLING THE POWER AND
HALVING THE EFFORT

YOU WILL FIND OUT THAT
THERE ARE ALL SORTS OF WAYS
OF LEARNING, NOT ONLY
FROM PEOPLE AND BOOKS BUT
FROM SHEER TRYING

FROM 'WOOD AND GARDEN' BY GERTRUDE JEKYLL

CHARACTERISTICS

Italic capitals are written with the same pen angle throughout. Like italic lowercase, they are based on the oval O and have a constant forward slant.

LETTER HEIGHT	PEN ANGLE	O FORM	SERIFS
8 nib widths.	45°.	The O is oval and in proportion to the lowercase italic o.	Oval hooks relating to the oval O for a basic version, but other serifs, such as those described for Roman capitals (p. 61), may be used.

STROKE ORDER AND DIRECTION	SPEED	SLANT	
These characteristics are the same as for Roman capitals.	Moderate.	Approximately 5° forward, as for lowercase italic.	

Skeleton letterforms

Like Roman capitals, italic capitals can be grouped according to their width. But because the letterforms are more compressed, their width differences are less marked. It is useful to recognize the width differences that do exist before writing the capitals in their weighted form. As with other scripts, skeleton forms are the basis of this study.

FORMATION GROUPS

Italic capitals fall into the same formation groups as Roman capitals, but based on the concept of the oval within the parallelogram instead of the circle within the square. The letters have a 5° forward slant.

Oval letters: O, Q, C, G, D. The C, G, and D are seven-eighth-width letters.

Three-quarter-width letters: H, A, V, N, T, U, X, Y, Z. These fit into a parallelogram that is three-quarters the width of the original one. The width has been reduced by one-eighth on each side to give an area approximately equal to that of the oval. The letters in this group are shown in two diagrams for clarity. They are all equal in width at their widest point.

Half-width letters: B, P, R, K, E, F, L, S, I, J. These are about half the width of the original parallelogram, except I and J, which are single-stroke letters. Most of the letters in this group are two-tier letters, based on two ovals inside parallelograms, the top tier slightly smaller than the bottom in height and width. S aligns at the front with the slight forward slant of the script; it is shown with J, which has the same base curve.

Wide letters: M and W. M fits into the original parallelogram. The central axis of the V part should have the same forward slant as the script. W consists of two V's of equal width, with the same slant.

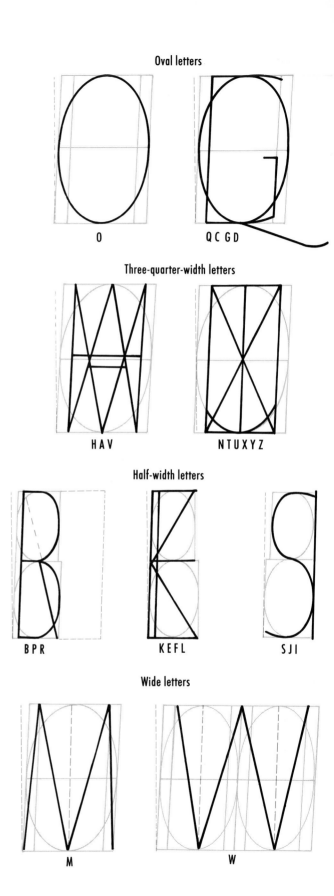

Oval letters

O   Q C G D

Three-quarter-width letters

H A V   N T U X Y Z

Half-width letters

B P R   K E F L   S J I

Wide letters

M   W

SKELETON PRACTICE

Practice writing the letters in pencil in their formation groups, paying particular attention to their relative widths. Numerals and arrows show the correct stroke order and direction. Refer to the Watchpoints box on page 98 for additional information, on letter construction. Remember to check spacing according to the Rule of Three (p. 25).

1 *Rule double lines ¾″ (18 mm) apart.*

2 *Write the letters in group order, as shown below, using an HB pencil. Follow the stroke order and direction indicated, and write on alternate lines.*

3 *Repeat each group as often as necessary, checking letter widths after each writing.*

4 *Try the alternative stroke order and direction shown for certain letters (see p. 97). Push strokes add continuity to V, W, and M, and make a neater follow-through from curve to base in B and D, but they are harder than pull strokes.*

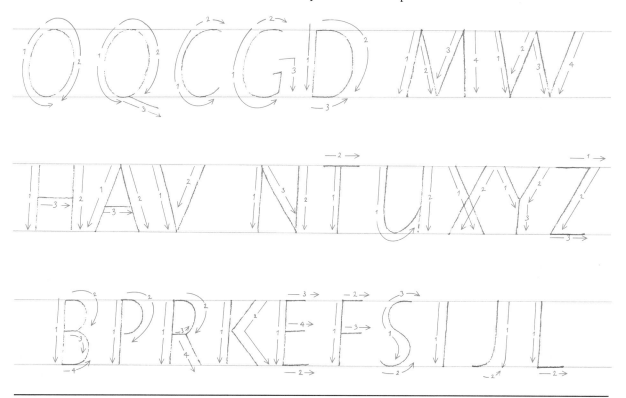

WRITING WORDS

Begin word practice as soon as you feel confident with the italic capital alphabet, in order to promote fluency.

1 *Write the words shown at right in pencil between lines ruled at ¾″ (18 mm). Copy letterform and spacing with care.*

2 *Rewrite each word as often as necessary.*

Weighted letterforms

Once you have mastered the basic skeleton forms, you can move on to the weighted versions of italic capitals. As with other scripts you will find it useful to do some work with double pencils, which clearly show the construction of the weighted letterforms. You will also need to give some attention to learning the serifs, which are responsible for much of the rhythm and fluidness of the script. They help the eye flow naturally from letter to letter along the line.

FREE ITALIC CAPITALS

Half-inch (13 mm) single and multiline pens were used with gouache color changes in the pen for this decorative piece.

PENCIL LETTERFORMS

Your first use of the weighted form could be with either double pencils or a carpenter's pencil as shown here. Pay particular attention to stroke joins as you practice.

1 *Sharpen your pencil to a width of $^3/_{16}$" (5 mm).*

2 *Rule lines $1^1/_2$" (4 cm) apart.*

3 *Keep the pencil edge at an angle of 45°, steepening further for the first stroke of M and uprights of N.*

4 *Copy the letters shown at right, referring to the alphabet on page 94 for additional information if necessary.*

SERIFS

A number of serifs are suitable for use with italic capitals, as shown at right. Oval hooks are the best to try first. They are simple to write and encourage flow and rhythm — unlike built-up serifs, which require pen lifts. Note that the built up top serifs shown at right are constructed before the downstroke is added. The downstroke thus provides a clean line from top to bottom, as well as completing the serifs.

Oval hook serif   Built-up triangular serif   Built-up slab serif

LETTER FORMATION GROUPS

Practice weighted letters first in their formation groups to establish accurate letter widths. Look at the alphabet details and checklist on page 98 before writing the formation groups, and check your letter-shapes closely against the examples as you practice.

1 *Write the groups as shown below between lines ruled at 8 nib widths of a Mitchell's No. 2 nib.*
2 *Use a pen angle of 45°, steepening to 50°–60° for the first stroke of M and the vertical strokes of N.*
3 *Practice each group several times, following the model closely.*
4 *Check the letters after each attempt, paying close attention to widths.*

SPACING

Establishing the space between the letters in the "H I O C" diagram will guide you toward even spacing with the broad pen. The spacing practiced here sets the pattern for all the italic capital work that follows.

1 *Write the italic capital H and place an I alongside it at a distance of two-thirds the width of the H counter.*
2 *Place an O slightly closer and a C even closer. Equal spacing depends on two straight-sided letters being farthest apart and two curved letters being closer.*

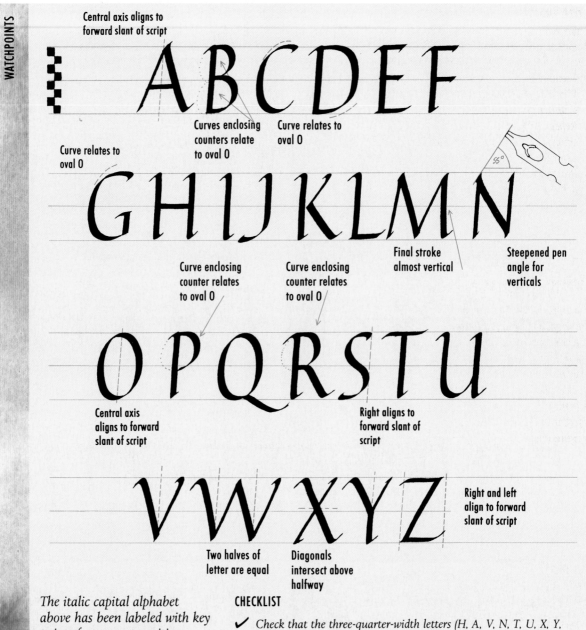

Central axis aligns to forward slant of script

Curves enclosing counters relate to oval O

Curve relates to oval O

Curve relates to oval O

Curve enclosing counter relates to oval O

Curve enclosing counter relates to oval O

Final stroke almost vertical

Steepened pen angle for verticals

Central axis aligns to forward slant of script

Right aligns to forward slant of script

Right and left align to forward slant of script

Two halves of letter are equal

Diagonals intersect above halfway

The italic capital alphabet above has been labeled with key points for accurate writing. Take note of these and read the checklist before you begin to write the alphabet. Rule your paper at 8 nib widths of a Mitchell's No. 2 nib and write the alphabet in sections: A–F, G–N, O–U, V–Z. Repeat each section several times, checking letter shapes and spacing each time before rewriting.

CHECKLIST

✔ Check that the three-quarter-width letters (H, A, V, N, T, U, X, Y, Z) are equal in width at their widest point, and not wider than O, Q, C, G or D.

✔ Make sure that the pen angle is steep enough for the first strokes of M and N, or the thin strokes will be too heavy.

✔ Maintain the correct forward slant in letters containing diagonals, especially M. Remember that the V part of these letters should have the same slant as the thick downstrokes of the script.

✔ Do not allow the final stroke of M to project too far to the right of the vertical or the letter will look too upright.

WORD PRACTICE

Begin writing these words as soon as you feel confident with the alphabet. Tackling the same few words at first will enhance your accuracy and readiness for unfamiliar letter groupings.

1 *Write at a letter height of 8 nib widths of a Mitchell's No. 2 nib.*

2 *Repeat each of the words shown several times, checking letterforms and spacing before rewriting.*

3 *Practice as many times as you need to achieve accuracy and rhythm.*

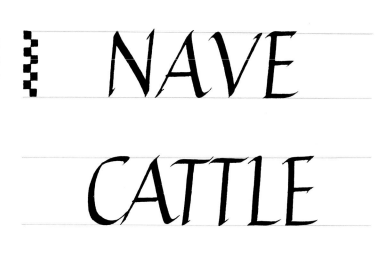

Using italic capitals

Plain italic capitals have a formal feeling. But this effect can be softened with the creative use of color. Here the lettering is written over a wash, giving the background the effect of a rainy morning. A Mitchell's No. 2 nib is used, and the finished lettering is in gouache.

1 *Write the entire text in ink on layout paper. Then cut up the words. After you finalize the design, paste up the words.*

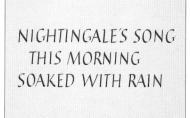

2 *Write the quotation on hot-pressed paper using gouache. This leaves a plain white background.*

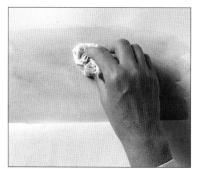

3 *Alternatively, add a wash to the paper. Once dry, cover with gum sandarac. This will help to sharpen the writing.*

4 *Write the lettering in gouache on top of the prepared wash, again following the original pasteup.*

Finished piece *The result looks formal, but the slight forward slant of the capitals gives a hint of movement, echoing the driving rain.*

DOWN IN SCALE

It is best to begin learning italic capitals in a large nib size, such as Mitchell's No. 1½ or 2, so that all the details of the letters are seen clearly. Once you have achieved accurate lettering and spacing at this size, move down in scale, but do so progressively, adjusting to each size in sequence. The diagram (right) shows some sample letters written in successively smaller nib sizes.

1 *Rule writing lines at 8 widths of the nib you are using.*
2 *Write the alphabet in progressively smaller nib sizes (Mitchell's No. 2½, 3, 3½, 4, 5).*

No. 2½ *OABCDE*

No. 3 *OABCDE*

No. 3½ *OABCDE*

No. 4 *OABCDE*

No. 5 *OABCDE*

Using italic capitals and lowercase

An interesting contrast can be made by using areas of text written in capital letters alongside those in lowercase. Here both sets of words are written with a Mitchell's No. 4 nib. With capitals, the lettering looks more dominant, lending weight to the words. The words in lowercase have a lighter effect.

1 *Try various designs in pencil thumbnails. This will help you work out which words should be in capitals and which in lowercase.*

2 *Write the words in ink on layout paper, then cut them up for use in making pasteups.*

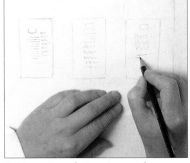

3 *Lay out individual words following the thumbnail sketch. Select line breaks and paste up the design.*

4 *Write the final version of the text following the pasteup.*

Finished piece *Using textured paper for the final draft lends a richer feeling to the work.*

STARK
WINTER
LANDSCAPE
STILL
AND
SILENT
SAVE THE
CRY OF
GULLS
OVER
FURROWS

*Birth
and rebirth
invisible
growing
in tree
plant
& beast
sunrise
of the
colors
of spring*

LARGE AND SMALL ITALIC CAPITALS

It is appropriate to write some texts entirely in capitals, and using more than one nib size will give you good practice in balancing different scales of writing. Ensure a standard letter height for each nib size you use, as shown in the example at right. You can also practice varying the standard letter weight to produce either light- or heavy-weight versions of this script with different nib sizes.

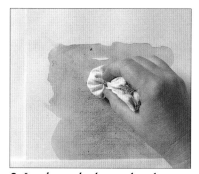

MIST·SHROUDED HILLS MUTED COLOURS STILL AIR OF AUTUMN AFTERNOON COOL AND SILENT· WEAK RAYS OF SUNLIGHT

Using large and small italic capitals

One way emphasis can be given to a piece of calligraphy is by using more than one nib size. Some experimentation is required to find suitable contrasts, in this instance, between two sizes of capitals. Here the small capitals are written using a Mitchell's No. 4 nib and the large capitals are written using a Mitchell's No. 2¹/₂.

1 *Write the two parts of the quotation in different nib sizes. Select contrasting sizes and paste them up.*

2 *Lay down a background wash on a heavy-weight paper. When this is dry, apply gum sandarac before writing.*

3 *Rule lines over the wash and write the lettering with gum ammoniac using the pasteup as a guide.*

4 *Apply gold leaf and burnish with a silk cloth. Gently brush off any additional gold.*

Finished piece *The gold lettering contrasts sharply with the background.*

WRITING LARGE

Large writing calls for sweeping hand and arm movements. It is a pleasure to feel large letters glide swiftly over the page. A text done with a plain stroke pen can be written without laborious planning.

1 *Practice a few words with a ³/₈″ (9 mm) plain stroke pen.*

2 *Keep the letters well-proportioned at a height of about 8 nib widths.*

3 *Practice first with ruled lines and then try writing freely, judging the height by eye.*

4 *Add color changes in the pen to vary the effect.*

Using large italic capitals

Large italic capitals can look very attractive. The pen used is a ³/₈″ (9 mm) border pen that produces just two lines — one thick and one thin. Using a split pen prevents large lettering from becoming too heavy. The space created between the two pen lines adds lightness.

1 Write the entire text in ink on layout paper. At this stage it is possible to experiment with several multilined border pens.

2 Lay out the words, fix the design and line breaks, then paste up the text.

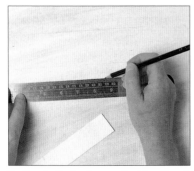

3 Create the background with a Conté crayon. Spray with fixative, rule up the paper, and then dust with gum sandarac (see p. 37).

4 Write the lettering with gum ammoniac. Apply the transfer gold leaf and burnish with a silk cloth.

5 Gently brush off the excess gold leaving the letters sharply distinct.

Finished piece *The combination of gold lettering over a blue and yellow gives an impression of sky and grass.*

THE
DANCE
OF THE
WINGING
BIRDS
AND THE
WAVING
GRASS

Cursive italic

MASTERING THE LETTERFORMS

Cursive means joined and flowing and can refer to any script written with few or no pen lifts. The letter joins, known as ligatures, are the product of writing with speed. In italic, they are diagonal or horizontal. The addition of ligatures alters the letter construction in many cases, and for this reason, cursive italic is treated as a separate script.

During the Renaissance many cursive italics were produced, each subtly different, depending on the style or choice of the individual scribe. It is one of the pleasures of calligraphy that each writer can bring a personal interpretation to the most familiar script. It is essential, however, to build such enhancements on a thorough knowledge of the basic features of the script.

The rich variety of Renaissance italics continues to provide today's calligraphers with a fertile ground for reference and experiment. But to learn the essential characteristics of cursive italic you must look at a script as free as possible from personal features. A cursive italic, with the same basic characteristics as formal italic but with the letters linked by ligatures, is the best starting point. For this script you will need to master two key strokes: the thin diagonal and the weighted horizontal.

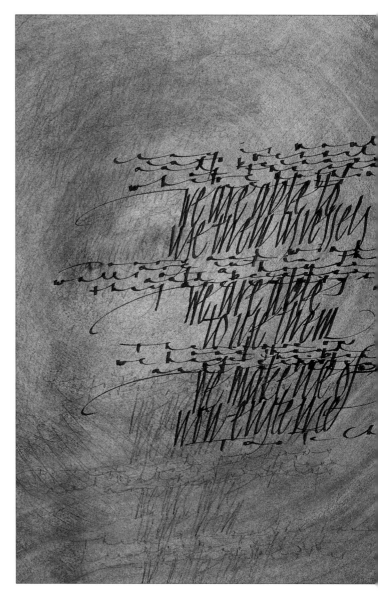

TAO TE CHING — Paivi Vesanto

This lively piece of cursive italic shows the use of contrast between narrow and extended letterforms and between heavy- and lightweight characters. The swirling colors of the pastel background add to the movement of the piece. Dimensions: 22" × 14" (55 cm × 35 cm).

BOG QUEEN — Julia Vance

This detail of a panel of poetry by Seamus Heaney shows a dancing cursive italic with flourishes and subtle italic capitals written in silver gouache over a pastel background. Dimensions: 51" × 11" (127 cm × 27.5 cm).

WEIGHTED HORIZONTAL STROKES

The weighted horizontal stroke is important for the tops of letters such as d, g, q, a, s, f. These letters may start with the top stroke, unlike formal italic. For speed and continuity, the stroke is pushed from right to left. In Renaissance times, these "lids" were often written with a pull from left to right followed by a push from right to left exactly over the first stroke. This was to avoid lifting the pen off the paper. It is a movement still used in some letter combinations, such as ma. At word beginnings, however, it is sufficient to start with a right to left push stroke. The alternative is to use the formal italic stroke order (see p. 84). The exercise at right enables you to try three different methods of writing horizontals and to decide which stroke sequence suits you.

1 Following the example above, try the three methods of writing the letter a.
2 Repeat each method of writing several times, and then use each of them in words of your choice.
3 You will probably find the first two methods more difficult, they involve push strokes against the front of the nib, but they eliminate pen lifts and ensure writing flow.

THIN DIAGONAL LIGATURES

The diagonal ligature is a thin uphill push stroke, shown as a broken line joining the serifs in the example at right. It is produced by moving the thin edge of the nib uphill diagonally to the right at a 45° angle. All diagonal joins are parallel.

Following the examples at right, practice the thin diagonals until you have achieved accurate flowing letterforms.
1 Rule your lines at 5 nib widths of a Mitchell's No. 2 nib.
2 Write the letters shown incorporating thin diagonal joins which are formed by pushing the nib uphill at an angle of 45°.
3 Check your writing, making sure that all diagonal joins are parallel.

USING LETTER JOINS

The various types of joins are shown at right and below.

Diagonal joins (type 1): These occur between letters with a lead-in or lead-out serif. These must be kept thin, straight, and parallel.

Diagonal joins (type 2): These lead from the base of letter bodies.

Horizontal joins: The ligature usually looks less heavy if it is written with a slight curve.

Double letters: These letters can be left unjoined, or joined with preceding diagonal ligatures.

Letters with descenders: Letters ending in a tail to the left are usually unjoined. A join may be added after lifting the pen to give continuity.

acdehi

Diagonal joins (type 1)

klmntu

beps

Diagonal joins (type 2)

forvwx *ff tt ff tt*

Horizontal joins   Double letters

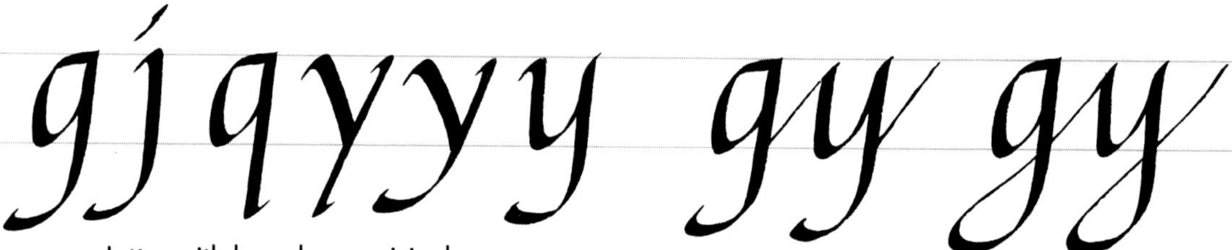

gj qyyy *gy gy*

Letters with descenders — unjoined

Letters with descenders — join after penlift

Letters with descenders — continuous join

PRACTICING LETTER JOINS

It is a good idea to practice cursive italic first by writing the alphabet with an m between each letter. Use lines ruled at an x height of 5 nib widths of a Mitchell's No. 2. (Note: The model below is reduced in size).

1 *Repeat the alphabet at least twice.*
2 *Check your letterforms, joins, and spacing, but concentrate on rhythm.*

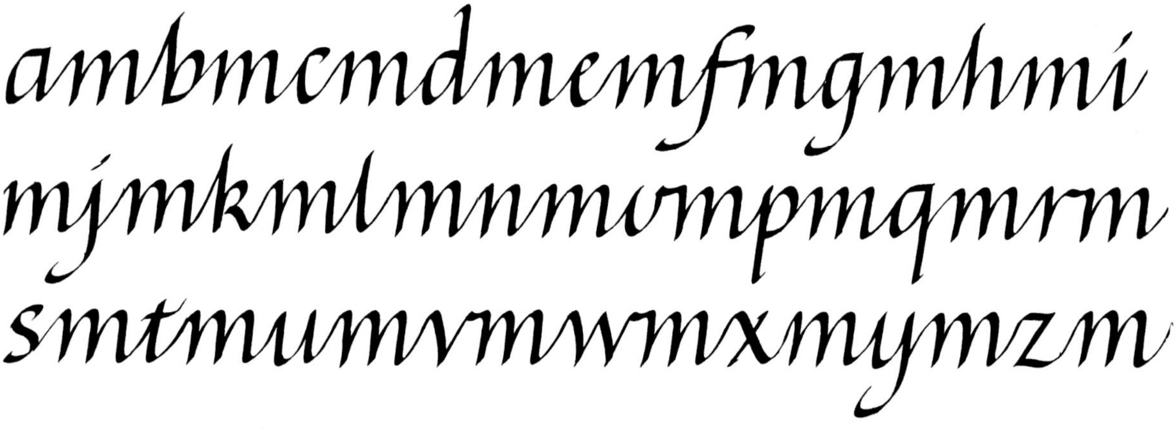

ambmcmdmemfmgmhmi

mjmkmlmnmompmqmrm

smtmumvmwmxmymzm

WRITING SMALL

The first exercises for cursive italic use a fairly large nib (Mitchell's No. 2), so that details of joins and letterforms can be seen clearly. However, smaller nibs are better adapted to the flow of this script. You may find it easier to develop a rhythm using a smaller nib.

1 *Use a Mitchell's No. 4 nib at an x height of 5 nib widths.*
2 *Write the words shown at right in this size.*
3 *Repeat the exercise until you feel at ease with the smaller nib.*

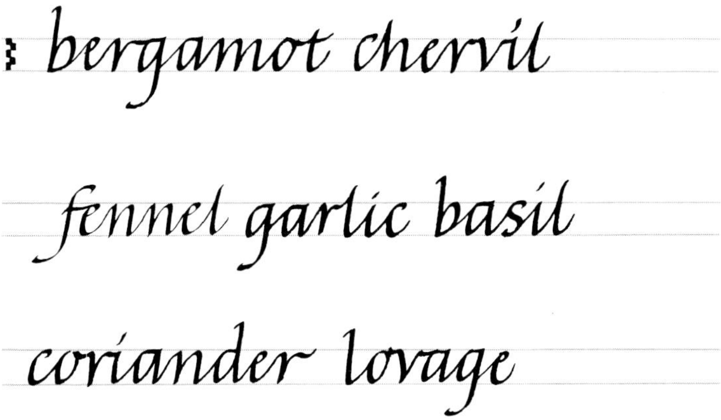

bergamot chervil

fennel garlic basil

coriander lovage

Using cursive script

Although cursive italic is often used for handwriting, it is also suitable for a wide range of calligraphic uses. Here it is used to render a quotation in gouache over a colored wash. A Mitchell's No. 4 nib is used throughout. The cursive hand is written at greater speed than formal italic, the joins drawing the eye naturally from letter to letter.

1 *Write the text in ink, then cut out and pasteup the words. This layout is copied in gouache.*

2 *To enliven the finished work, add flourishes (see pp. 108–113) to some letters in the main text.*

3 *Cut out and add the trial flourishes to the layout. The exact positioning of elaborate ascenders and descenders can be critical.*

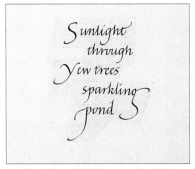

4 *The effect of the layout should be balanced and harmonious.*

The finished work *uses gold leaf lettering over a watercolor wash. For further information on applying gold leaf, see p. 101.*

Flourishes & swashes

The embellishment of letters with ornamental flourishes goes back to the Renaissance. The manuals of the Renaissance writing masters contain a wealth of inventive flourishes. Although the term suggests flamboyance, flourishes can range from subtle stroke extensions to elaborate traceries of loops and lines. They can be a wonderful enhancement to calligraphic work, provided they are carefully matched to their context. Sign writing, commemorative inscriptions, diplomas, and greeting cards are just some of the areas in which they can be used with a restrained or spirited effect.

Flourishes must appear to be an intrinsic part of the letter, not a contrived addition. They need to be written with flowing movement, speed, directness — and good pen control. In the enthusiasm for writing flourishes, it is easy to neglect the letter shapes themselves. These must be accurate if letter and flourish are to form a harmonious whole.

Some people take rapidly to writing flourishes, but whether you find flourishes easy or not, you must first understand the principles of good flourish design. Remember that the choice of flourish depends on the design context and the purpose of the calligraphy. Begin by learning some basic flourish shapes, but also study the creative ideas of other calligraphers, past and present. Look for inspiration in the imaginative flourishes of such Renaissance calligraphers as Arrighi, Tagliente, and Palatino, which you can find in illustrated books, and in the work of accomplished 20th-century calligraphers, who have developed innovative lettering for contemporary needs.

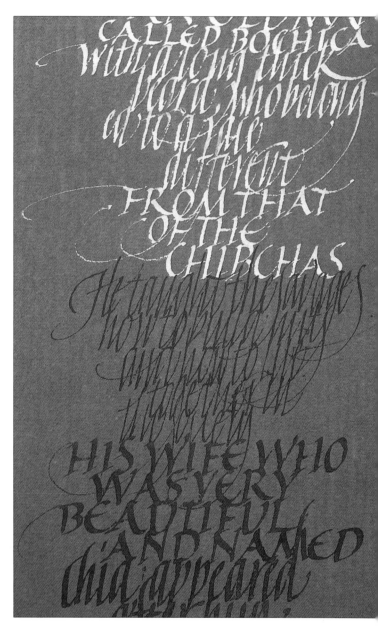

POETRY PANEL — Paivi Vesanto

Elegant flourishes form a natural part of these freely written italics and italic capitals.

108

FLOURISHED CAPITALS

Because of their role in titles and at text beginnings, capitals are usually the first letterforms to be considered when learning flourish design.

You can add flourishes to the entire capital alphabet with the aid of four basic flourish types. These are shown below. Each flourish is complete. Each group begins with a simple flourish and progresses to more complex variations. Acquire a basic repertoire of flourishes by practicing the direction groups below.

1 *Rule lines ¹/₄" (6 mm) apart, the equivalent of 8 nib widths of a Mitchell's No. 4 nib.*

2 *Use a pencil at first, so that your hand and arm are not restrained by the resistance of the broad nib against the paper. With practice, this resistance should not be a problem.*

3 *Loosen up with some large, sweeping movements, such as the tail on the R. Let the pencil move lightly over the paper.*

4 *Copy flourishes from each group, in the order shown, until you have memorized them well enough to write without hesitation.*

5 *When you feel confident with your pencil, repeat the exercise with a No. 4 nib.*

6 *You may need to make several attempts at each flourish to produce flowing lines.*

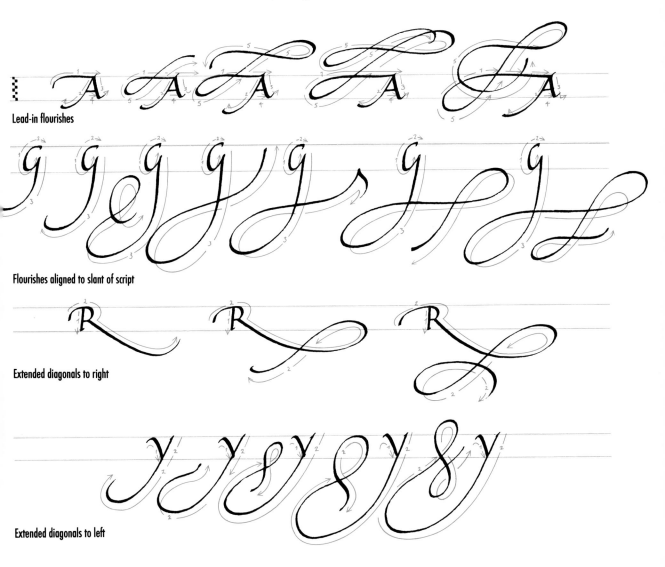

Lead-in flourishes

Flourishes aligned to slant of script

Extended diagonals to right

Extended diagonals to left

SWASH CAPITALS

Swash capitals are relatively simple flourished letters that are ideally suited to line beginnings — for instance, in poetry. The alphabet on the right provides a good starting point for beginners. To write these letters with both flow and control, copy the alphabet, following the stroke order and direction indicated.

1 *Rule lines to a height of 8 nib widths of a Mitchell's No. 2 nib.*

2 *Practice the capitals in alphabetical order, writing each letter several times before moving on to the next letter.*

3 *Take care with letterspacing, so that swashes do not overlap.*

4 *When you have gained in confidence, try some swash capitals in a text of your choice.*

FLOURISHES FOR LOWERCASE ITALIC

Flourish design for lowercase italic follows the same principles as for capitals. There are two main directions in which the extension can travel. At right you will find examples for y and h, moving from a simple flourish to more complex designs.

Practice flourishes for italic minuscules with the designs for y and h shown.

1 *Rule lines $^3/_{16}$" (5 mm) apart, the correct x height for a Mitchell's No. 4 nib.*

2 *Practice each letter several times in pencil until you are familiar with the design.*

3 *Repeat the exercise using a Mitchell's No. 4 nib, omitting any flourishes that are too difficult at first.*

4 *Make sure that the reservoir moves easily up and down the nib, or the pen will not move easily over the paper.*

D E F F G H

K L L M N N

Q R S T U V

W X Y Y Z

h h h h h h h h

y y y y y y y

EXPERIMENTING WITH FLOURISH DESIGN

Once you are familiar with some basic flourishes, try making your own designs. Planning in pencil or felt-tip pen will enable you to work faster and more freely.

1 *Write spontaneously, letting the ideas flow.*
2 *Follow up with design refinements using the broad-nibbed pen.*

FLOURISH EXPERIMENT
In this decorative piece of work, carefully planned flourishes connect the spaces and carry the eye into the design.

FLOURISHED PANEL
Lawrence R. Brady

This panel, produced as part of a corporate identity program, uses carefully considered flourishes at the top and bottom. These flowing strokes help to integrate the different elements in the design.

CHECKLIST FOR IMPROVISED FLOURISHES

✔ *Spontaneous flourishes depend on knowledge and pen control.*
✔ *Write flourishes smoothly and rhythmically. Speed develops with practice.*
✔ *Write flourishes continuously. It is necessary to break them into component strokes only when writing with a very large nib, and not always then.*
✔ *Where straight lines and curves join, make sure the transition follows through in a fluid movement.*
✔ *Establish a sense of spaciousness around the letter. Overclose flourishes create a cramped design.*
✔ *Diagonal strokes are usually parallel. Do not write them too close together, or the flourish will look heavy.*
✔ *Design and practice flourishes in pencil for uninhibited movement and speed.*
✔ *Practice with chisel-edged brushes or large chisel-edged felt-tip markers to loosen arm movement and encourage experimentation.*

Using flourishes

Flourishes should be carefully proportioned and must relate to, and not obscure, other parts of the text. Sometimes a flourished design may be complete in its own right. For a certificate, poster, title page, or dust jacket like the one shown here, only a decorative heading or panel may be needed, with plenty of space all around it. This gives you more scope for flourishing.

1 *Much of the success of flourishing comes from detailed planning of the design. Here preliminary pencil roughs are sketched.*

2 *When first learning to design flourishes it may help to pencil the flourishes onto the simple letterforms written in ink.*

3 *Several different flourish designs are written using a Mitchell's No. 2 nib. Each design is then considered within the context.*

4 *The final design is written in gouache, and a decorative border is added in gouache with a brush.*

5 *The paper is then trimmed to the dimensions of the book, leaving a flap 1" (2.5 cm) wide on each end that folds inside the cover.*

AMPERSANDS

Symbols other than standard letterforms may also be flourished or written in unusual ways. An example is the sign for "and" known as an ampersand. An ampersand must harmonize with the script being written, and a simple design may suit the context better than a flamboyant one. Three examples of ampersands suitable for use with contemporary calligraphy are shown at right, together with the stroke sequences for writing them.

1 *Rule lines to a height of 8 nib widths of a Mitchell's No. 2 nib.*

2 *Practice each of the ampersands in turn, first on their own and afterward in context with an appropriate script.*

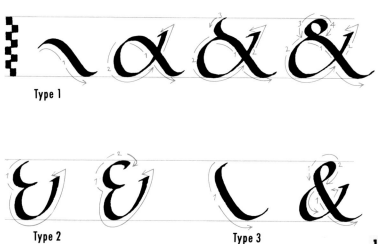

Type 1

Type 2   Type 3

Versals

Versals are built up capitals, each part of which consists of freely drawn compound strokes. In medieval times they were used to draw the reader's eye to headings, important sections of text, or verse beginnings. The finest examples of pure letterforms are from the Carolingian period of the 9th and 10th centuries. These graceful letterforms reflect the proportions of the Roman inscriptional capitals on which they were based.

Today, versals are useful for titles and for interpretive work with prose and poetry. They can be used in their classical forms or with variations in height, weight, slant, or letter width that give scope for exploration.

MEDIEVAL MANUSCRIPT

This early medieval manuscript shows the traditional use of versals for introductory text and for illuminated letters.

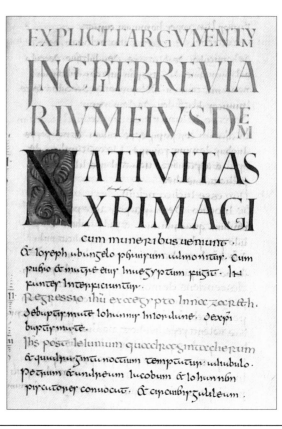

CONSTRUCTION

Versals are built stroke by stroke using a technique that is close to drawing. The thick compound strokes, which are a major feature, consist of two slightly curved outer strokes, filled with a final single stroke.

Because they have their origins in Roman capitals, the best preparation for learning versals is to practice skeleton Roman capitals in pencil as shown on page 67 at a height of ³⁄₄″ (2 cm). Then try the basic component strokes shown below and on the facing page: thick verticals, thick diagonals, thin diagonals, curves, thin verticals, and thin horizontals. Practice each stroke with a Mitchell's No. 4 nib on lines ruled at 24 nib widths. Then try the sample letter that incorporates that stroke.

Thin verticals

1 *Hold the nib edge at a 0° pen angle and draw a horizontal top serif.*

2 *Maintaining the same pen angle, draw a vertical downstroke.*

3 *Add a shaping stroke and horizontal serif at termination.*

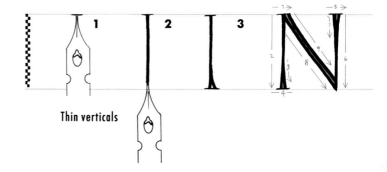

Thin verticals

Thick verticals

1 *Draw a horizontal top serif as before.*

2 *Maintaining the same pen angle (0°), draw the left downstroke with a slight curving inward.*

3 *Leave a gap of 1 nib width, and draw the right downstroke, also curving inward. The form should be heaviest at the top.*

4 *Place the nib at the top of the gap and pull the ink down to fill the gap. Finish with a horizontal stroke, completing the bottom serif.*

Thin diagonals

1 *Draw a horizontal top serif as before.*

2 *With the nib at 90° to the stroke direction, draw a downward diagonal.*

3 *Finish with a shaping stroke and a horizontal serif.*

Thick diagonals

1 *Draw a horizontal top serif as before.*

2 *With the nib at 90° to the stroke direction, draw the left downward diagonal.*

3 *Continue as for thick verticals (above).*

Horizontal arms

1 *Hold the nib edge at 90° to the horizontal, and pull it to the right.*

2 *Add flaring with a shaping stroke between the main stroke and the serif.*

3 *Maintaining the 90° pen angle, add a vertical serif at termination.*

Curves

1 *Start with a pen angle of about 15° to the horizontal to give slight weight to the thinnest parts of the curved letters, at top and bottom. Draw the inside curve first.*

2 *Add the outside curve with a 0° pen angle. The distance between the two curves should be 1 nib width at its widest point — half way up the letter height.*

3 *Fill the gap.*

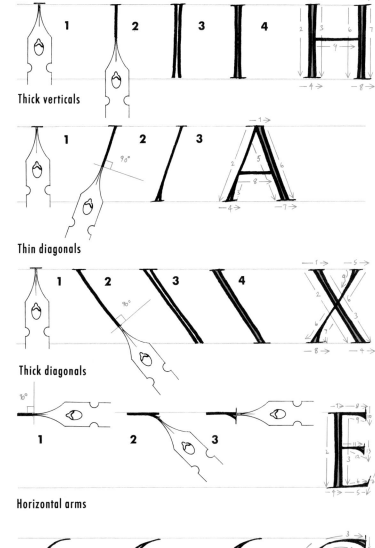

Thick verticals

Thin diagonals

Thick diagonals

Horizontal arms

Curves

SPACING

Versals are elegant letters, provided that their weight is not exaggerated and they are accurately spaced. Overclose or erratic spacing destroys the effect. Use the "H I O C" diagram (right) to establish the correct spacing pattern before practicing the alphabet. Practice the diagram, checking the spacing by eye.

Circular outer
curves

Added stroke at
termination

Oval bottom
counter

Gradual
transition from
straight to
curved strokes

Added stroke at
termination

Added stroke at
termination

Aligned at
right, serif
nearly half way
up the letter
height

Horizontal just
over half way
up letter height

Slight thinning
at mid-point

Gradual
transition from
straight to
curved strokes

Vertical letter with
counters equal width

Vertical axis

Curve meets
stem half way
up the letter
height

Bowl joins stem
nearly half way
up the letter
height

Circular
counters

Aligned
vertically at
left and right

Gradual
transition
from thick
vertical to
curve

Slight thinning
at center of
thick diagonals

Crosses slightly
above half way
up the letter height

Diagonals meet
half way down
the letter height

After practicing the
components of versals and
the H, I, O, C spacing
diagram, try writing the
alphabet. The component
strokes of versal letters are
assembled in the same order
as the individual strokes of
Roman capitals (see p. 66).

CHECKLIST

✔ Make sure that all thick verticals and diagonals measure 3 nib widths.

✔ Base your letter proportions on skeleton Roman capitals (p.66).

✔ Thick components should not be heavy or overshaped. The first two
strokes should be almost parallel with minimal inward curving.

✔ Hold the nib at 90° to make horizontals 1 nib width wide. Left-
handers will probably need to hold the nib at about 45°, widening the
stroke with an additional stroke.

✔ Do not overstate the flaring at the open ends of thin strokes.

✔ Check that serifs are fine, and not too long.

✔ Make sure that the outside of a curved letter is round.

✔ Check that the fullest point of a curve equals or slightly exceeds the
width of a thick stem.

Using versals

Although versals are formal, they can be used in many creative ways. This example, written in white gouache on a colored paper or background, is particularly delicate.

1 *First write the full text in versals in black ink on layout paper. Here a Mitchell's No. 4 nib is used.*

2 *Cut and paste the text. Try various layouts before deciding on a design.*

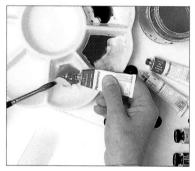

3 *Prepare the color washes, blend the colors and try them on the same kind of paper to be used for the final work.*

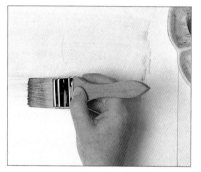

4 *When you are satisfied with the colors, apply the wash.*

5 *When the wash is completely dry, rule the paper following the selected layout. Prepare the surface with gum sandarac (p. 37).*

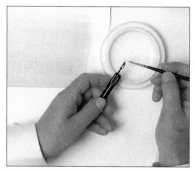

6 *Write the text in white gouache over the wash. Load the paint into the pen using a brush.*

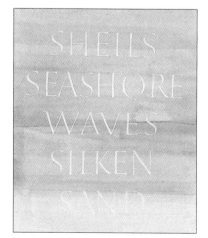

7 *The bands of colored wash look like sand, sea, and sky, reflecting the text.*

8 *An alternative finished version uses lettering in gold.*

Color and image

What is color?

COLOR AND IMAGE

Darkly inked letters on a white page, with their balance of contrast, shape, and texture, can be the perfect choice for a piece of work. But as traditional scribes knew, color can add character and substance and widen the opportunity for self-expression. In creative work especially, color, word, and image can work together to convey a theme, express a mood, emphasize an interesting surface, or explore an idea. Color may come from paper, ink, paint, colored pencil, pastel, or another material. It may be applied to a single letter, to a border, or over an entire design. It may be restrained or elaborate, a subtle background, a glimmering highlight, or a joyous outpouring. Its appropriateness and success will depend on your knowledge of the materials and understanding of how to combine them with text, script, and layout. The best way to start is by considering what color is.

ASPECTS OF COLOR

When working with color it is important to be aware of the different qualities of the colors we see and how these qualities can be incorporated into a work of calligraphy by the use of different color media. Our appreciation of color is governed by the eye's reaction to light of different wavelengths enabling us to distinguish between the colors of the spectrum — red, orange, yellow, green, blue, indigo, and violet. The vast range of colors that our eyes can register is produced by different mixtures of these wavelengths. Similarly, the pigments used in paints can be mixed in different ways to produce colors with precise characteristics. On the following pages examples of colors in nature are shown alongside painted examples to demonstrate sources of inspiration for color choices in your calligraphy.

IN MAY AND JUNE ⁝ COME PINKS OF ALL SORTS ⁝ ESPECIALLY THE BLUSH PINK; ⁝ ROSES OF ALL KINDS.

IDEAS FOR COLOR

One way of selecting colors for your work is to draw inspiration from nature. Here a palette of colors is derived from the picture of a flower. Do not just pick the obvious ones. The more subtle combinations will give you a wider working vocabulary. Test the colors on the paper you are going to be using before starting the work.

THE COLOR WHEEL

Exciting colors can be found in tubes or pans, but by mixing colors yourself you can greatly increase your options. A useful basis for experimentation is the color circle, or wheel, which provides a structured guide to the functions and relationships of color (below).

Red, yellow, and blue are the primary, or basic, colors from which others can be derived. The secondary colors are those produced by mixing the primary colors: orange (from red and yellow), green (from yellow and blue), violet (from blue and red). A mixture of all three primary colors makes gray. The tertiary colors are created by mixing equal proportions of a primary color and its adjacent secondary on the color wheel. Three primaries therefore produce three secondaries, and these together produce six tertiaries, giving a color wheel of a dozen hues.

Careful control over the proportions of each color used is important both to achieve a successful result and to be able to repeat it. It also helps to give you clear color ideas when planning a design. Making your own color wheel will give you the basic knowledge you need to mix colors successfully. You can also practice controlling proportions by choosing two primaries and mixing them to make a color scale that moves in graduated steps from one color to another — for example, from blue through purple to red. Keep notes and examples of various mixtures for future reference.

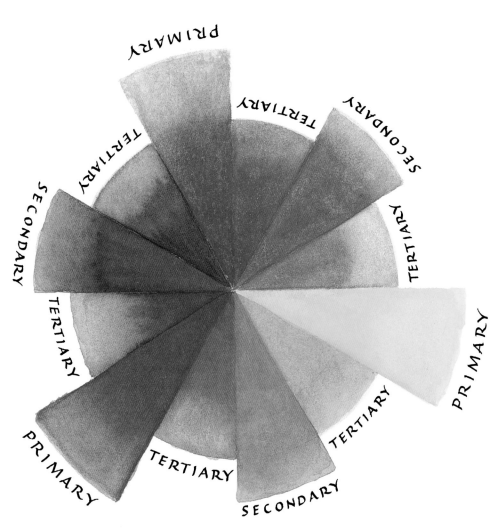

MAKING YOUR OWN COLOR WHEEL
Investigate the color possibilities of three primary colors by making your own color wheel. In addition to creating nine additional colors from the three primaries, within each segment you can achieve further variations by using paint at different dilutions, producing different degrees of opacity.

VALUE

Each basic color, or hue, has either light or dark value. For example, yellows have a lighter value than blues. The value of a particular color can generally be lightened by dilution and darkened by being mixed in a higher concentration.

COLOR TEMPERATURE

Color temperature helps to create mood, space, and the appearance of modeling. Warm colors seem to advance, and cool colors to recede. Colors are categorized as warm by association with the sun or fire, and this quality is evoked by rich yellows, reds, and colors adjacent to these. Cool colors are associated with ice, water, and sky, and include shades of blue, violet, and some greens.

Most colors can be made warmer or cooler by adding warm or cool pigments, red-orange being the exception. Placing cooler colors beside warmer ones heightens the sense of coolness or warmth.

COMPLEMENTARY COLORS

These are positioned directly opposite each other on the color wheel. Mixed in equal quantities they neutralize each other, resulting in grays. A small quantity of color has a slightly dulling effect when added to its complement. The juxtaposition of complementaries creates vibration, which is why orange letters on blue do not read easily.

ANALOGOUS COLORS

These are colors adjacent to each other on the color wheel — yellow, yellow-green, and green, for example. They are used to create mood and temperature and to enhance harmony.

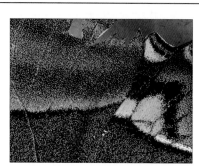

Light

Dark

Warm colors

Cool colors

Complementary colors

Analogous colors

BUYING PAINT

The first colors you will need to buy are the three primaries in either gouache or watercolor. There are many brands and blends of red, yellow, and blue, and each of these will produce a different hue. This is because primary pigments have a natural (or manufactured) bias toward one of the secondary colors. For example, ultramarine blue has a tendency toward violet, and cerulean blue toward green; cadmium red is a red-orange, and alizarin crimson has a violet tinge, cadmium yellow has an orange hue, and lemon yellow is slightly green. This color bias will affect your attempts to mix a "pure" range of secondaries and tertiaries. When making your first color wheel, you should look for middle-range primaries with the least tendency toward the secondary colors of orange, violet, or green.

For a basic palette it is advisable to have two reds, two blues, and two yellows, each containing an opposite color bias. This will give you a varied and reliable working range of pigments. Remember that watercolor produces a more transparent color than gouache. The choice of paint type will therefore depend on the effect you want.

Cadmium yellow

Lemon yellow

Cadmium red

Alizarin crimson

Ultramarine

Cerulean blue

KEEPING COLOR NOTES

It is a good idea to keep a folder of color examples and notes on how you mixed them. These will be your reference for subsequent matching and planning, helping you to visualize similar or alternative color choices and stimulating new ideas. Use the folder also for photographs or clippings showing colors or color combinations that appeal to you and pieces of material, leaves, paper wrappers, labels, or any other item whose colors catch your eye and which you might use for inspiration.

123

Using color

A colored background applied to the paper for calligraphy may create a textured effect or stand as a unified tone "washed" over the entire surface. Adding this colour involves water, which may cause the fibers in the paper to swell and the sheet to wrinkle as it dries. The larger the surface, the more prone it is to wrinkling. One way to avoid wrinkling is to use a heavy paper. A weight of 140 lb or so is suitable for most purposes, but if a large amount of water is used, a 200-lb or 300-lb paper may be needed. Lighter papers will resist wrinkling if they are stretched before use (see instructions on the facing page).

A background built with individual brushstrokes separately applied will show streaks and variations of color where the paint overlaps and dries irregularly. This method could be used to create texture. More often, however, you will want the subtler all-over effect achieved by "laying a wash." Methods for applying and blending washes are shown on the following pages.

Once you have developed the skill of laying a wash, you can achieve many exciting variations and textures. There is just one caution: bear in mind that you are going to write on the surface. If the background paint is too thick, paint from the pen will spread into it, blurring the writing, or you may be unable to write properly at all. So keep the paint thin under the area where you intend to write.

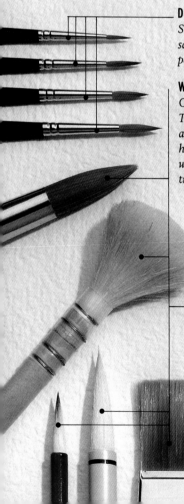

DETAIL BRUSHES
Should be springy red sable with well-pointed tips.

WASH BRUSHES
Can be round or flat. They should be soft and capable of holding plenty of water. A well pointed tip is helpful.

A single color in the pen may be transparent or opaque. By starting with one color in the pen and gradually introducing a second color as you reload the pen, you can create an interesting gradated effect. The pen can also create a broken succession of marks that contrast with areas of solid color in background washes. You could create tonal changes: light to dark or dark to light, or repeated sequences of light and dark. Variations can be introduced through different nib sizes or textural effects.

Papers that are to receive a watercolor background may need to be stretched before use to prevent them from wrinkling. For this you will need a rigid board (such as a drawing board) larger than the sheet to be stretched and some gummed brown paper tape.

1 Trim your paper so that there is at least 1½" (4 cm) leeway on all sides of the board. Choose which side of the paper is to be the work surface.

2 Immerse the paper in cold water in a sink or other suitably sized container for a minute or two. Alternatively, wet the paper under cold running water.

3 Lift the paper carefully and allow the excess water to drain from one corner. Take care not to rub water across the surface of the wet paper, which may damage the fibers, causing uneven paint effects.

4 Lay the paper on the board gently. Cut eight strips of gummed tape slightly longer than the sides of the sheet — two for each side. Wet the tape with a sponge.

5 Apply a tape strip along each edge of the paper so that it overlaps by about ¼" (6 mm). Smooth it down to attach it to the board. Repeat with the remaining strips. Set the board aside to dry.

LAYING A WASH

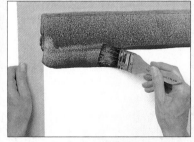

1 Use stretched paper still attached to the board. Work with the board slightly tilted. Load a thick, flat brush with paint, and apply horizontal strokes across the board. Allow each brushstroke to overlap the last.

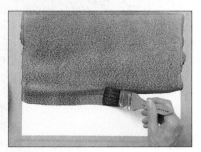

2 Continue to work down the paper, reloading the brush at the end of a stroke, not halfway through. Keep the strokes smooth and even. Do not try to rework a stroke that may not be perfect — this is liable to make matters worse.

3 When you finish laying the flat wash, the overlaps should gently blend together, leaving a flat field of background color.

BLENDING TWO COLORS

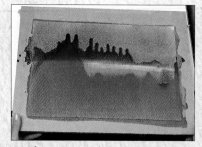

1 *Apply two colors — one from the top, the other from the bottom — on the stretched paper as if they were flat washes (see p. 125). The paper and board should be flat. It may help to wet the paper first.*

2 *The amount of overlap between the two colors can vary along the join. Let them bleed into each other.*

3 *The crossover of color can be controlled by tipping the board, first in one direction, then in another.*

BLENDING SEVERAL COLORS

1 *Try applying several washes to the stretched paper with a wide brush.*

2 *You do not have to lay the colors in simple strips — they can bleed and overlap freely.*

3 *To bleed the colors, tilt the paper and board until the colors run into one another.*

WET INTO WET

1 *For an effective way of making a mood-evoking background that does not distract from the calligraphy, apply areas of gouache over a wash that is still wet.*

2 *The wet gouache bleeds into the background wash, blurring the edges, which creates a soft, blended effect.*

3 *By dabbing the surface with tissue paper, you can control the bleed and in this way mold the finished effect.*

MULTICOLOR SPLATTER

1 For another way of producing an interesting color background, try splattering the stretched paper with paint.

2 Use a stencil brush that is loaded with paint, and flick it with the tip of your thumb. You can use more than one color.

3 Remember to wear old clothes when you do this, as spots of color fly everywhere. Limit the number of colors you use in any one area, or the result will look muddy.

MASKING FLUID RESIST

1 Apply masking fluid to stretched paper with a paintbrush. Rub off any unwanted fluid with your finger.

2 When the masking fluid is dry, lay your colored washes over it.

3 Once the color is dry, rub away the masking fluid with your finger, exposing the white of the paper.

ALTERNATIVE MATERIALS

Backgrounds treated with colored pencils, watercolor pencils, or pastels make an interesting alternative to colored paper or paint.

Colored pencils should be used with minimal pressure. To strengthen the tone, build up layers of light strokes, one on top of the other or use crosshatching.

Watercolor pencils are available in hard or soft grades and should be chosen to match your paper. A soft pencil is suitable for a soft paper, whose fibers could be torn by a hard point. A good way to use watercolor pencils is to work the color onto your paper from the pencils and then brush water over the colored surface. Conté pastels and those made from dry pigment and gum tragacanth or similar mixtures also produce exciting background effects.

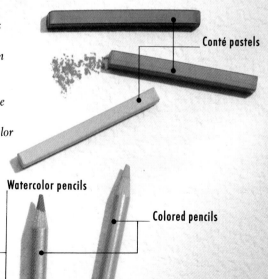

Conté pastels

Watercolor pencils

Colored pencils

127

Interpreting the text

COLOR AND IMAGE

The mood and meaning of the text will suggest the choice of color, design, and letterform. Aspects to consider include the sense and inflection of the words, associated connotations, and the use of contrasts. These have parallels in color terms. Tonal changes and use of the analogous range (p. 122) — for example, moving progressively from blue to green — create color harmony. This is also a good method of invoking mood and warmth or coolness.

Explore color considerations during the layout stage of a design (p. 48). Paint your color choices on tracing paper, which you can place over the layout and adjust as necessary.

It is wise to keep your colors understated at first and to work from light to dark. Color immediately attracts the eye, and bright colors will appear to come forward off the page. This can be helpful in enlivening a design or adding judiciously chosen emphasis. The eye's unconscious tendency to travel around a layout, linking like colors, can also be used to create unity. But color can easily be overdone, and it should therefore be approached with caution.

Visualizing color as mass and the lines of text as strands to be linked compatibly with it can help you assess suitable contrasts. For example, if the text suggests liveliness and activity, contrast this with a calmer background to avoid a muddled effect.

Elements such as verticals and horizontals can also create contrasts and tensions. A design can be strengthened by emphasizing these. The text itself, being a linear form, may be written vertically or horizontally, or compressed and angled to intensify tensions. To relax this tension, spread the verticals or horizontals farther apart.

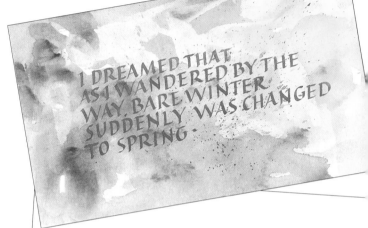

CONTROLLING COLOR
One rough idea for this quote suggests winter colors giving way to warmer tones (top). Another shows the lifting of winter gloom (middle). A third moves from winter to spring in a monochromatic progression (above).

Ideas for the dynamics of design — structure, layout, color, pattern, texture, rhythm, and mood — are most readily found in the environment. Look keenly at the world around you, analyzing it in visual terms and training your eye to seek out patterns, harmonies, and juxtapositions of texture, line, and color. Here a starfish, grass shoots, thorns, and woven rushes illustrate contrasting design possibilities. Practice interpreting what you see in terms of color and design. Record your observations in notes, sketches, or photographs — putting together a valuable source of stimulation for design ideas.

COLOR AND DESIGN

The design for a piece of colored calligraphy should be started with a number of thumbnail sketches.

1 The quote mentions leaping, which suggests a vertical design.

2 But trout do not leap in a regular fashion, so an asymmetrical design is tried.

3 However, a combined vertical and horizontal layout works better.

4 The design is refined, and the color of the background is developed. The finished work combines the splash of the leaping trout with the peaceful colors of the woodland and water.

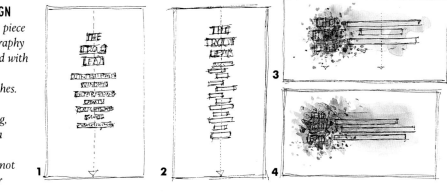

THE TROUT LEAPS

WINTER'S HARSH WIND HAS DEPARTED: WOODLAND IS BRIGHT: WATER FRUITFUL: PEACE IMMENSE:

129

WORDS AND ILLUSTRATION

Whether you use color or not, any image you choose should augment the meaning of the words. Text and image should be visually harmonious. Decisions on how to blend the two take place when you make thumbnail sketches or at the layout stage.

It is important to consider the overall space in which image and text appear and not to use decorative letters or illustrations merely as space fillers. The "negative" areas — those which are left free — are as essential to balanced layout as the positive ones. It is the shapes of spaces and marks together that make up the design. An image or illustration also contains negative areas, and these should be given equal consideration.

CHOOSING A FOCAL POINT

Begin by choosing a focal point: the part of your layout to which the eye will be guided first. You could feature this as a larger, darker, lighter, or more colorful letter, word, or image. You could establish an "active" area in which greater numbers of shapes or letters are closely gathered. Or you could draw, write, or paint an especially vigorous textural or visual element.

It is usually best to work from the focal point, so that no other text or image competes with it. If you establish two equally active areas, for example, the eye will look from one to the other, separating the design into rival parts. This does not mean that you cannot use another focal point, but that the second one should be more muted and should enhance the strength and direction of the main focus.

The position of the focal point needs to be carefully chosen. In the exact center of the design, it may look too obvious and therefore uninteresting. Too near the edge of the page, it may seem about to slip off. If it links too powerfully with another part of the design, it may divide the paper. In the same way, the text and the image should not divide the surface equally. If each occupies half the sheet, for example, the design is likely to be monotonous. Using too many colors steals attention from the image and the words. Intense color should not be used on insignificant detail.

There can be many sources of ideas for calligraphic composition and illustration. Get into the habit of looking at the environment around you and taking notes on interesting colors, textures, and objects that could be used in your work. Keep a scrapbook of these notes. Sketch in ideas for layouts, paste in photographs you find interesting, and use it for color and letterform observations.

SEEING NEGATIVE SHAPES

Try to see each of your layouts in terms of the negative areas it creates. These shapes are an essential part of the design. The layouts at left are shaded to draw attention to the negative areas they create.

If you decide to fill a negative area with an illustration, be sure to check that this does not alter the balance of the design.

DETERMINING THE FOCAL POINT

The focal point is the point of the image to which the eye is first drawn. Here the left-of-center focal point is determined by the area of darkest color in the background wash.

FOCAL POINT WITH WORDS AND IMAGE

Always ensure that the words and the image work together to reinforce the focal point. In this rough design, the left-of-center text placement is balanced by the extension of the wash to the right. This ensures that the focal point in the darkest wash area is maintained.

Focal point links foreground, middle ground, and sky

Passive middle ground balances relative activity of foreground and sky

THERE'S A WHISPER DOWN THE FIELD, WHERE THE YEAR HAS SHOT HER YIELD. AND THE RICKS STAND GREY TO THE SUN, SINGING, 'OVER THEN, COME OVER, FOR THE BEE HAS QUIT THE CLOVER, YOUR ENGLISH SUMMER'S DONE.'

A FINISHED COMPOSITION

In this piece of illustrated calligraphy, the composition was carefully planned around the focal point formed by the flock of birds. The furrows of the plowed field draw the eye across the text in the foreground to this point. This diagonal movement also provides a link across the horizontal divisions of the sky and landscape.

Use of color enhances the unity of the composition, with the purple-brown of the text echoing both the browns of the fields and the indigo of the sky.

Placement of text helps to emphasize foreground detail

Diagonal sweep of furrows draws eye toward focal point

131

Projects

Invitation

PROJECTS

Formal invitations can be greatly enhanced by calligraphy, used alone or combined with type. Handwritten letters and simple letter decoration — usually by means of flourishing (see pp. 108–113) — can add the individual touch that type alone lacks.

Formal scripts, such as italic, are suitable for occasions such as weddings, christenings, or banquets, but there are no hard-and-fast rules. The invitation could be written entirely in capitals, or in areas of upper- and lowercase letters to suit the text and overall design. You might combine compatible scripts, use a suitably embellished capital, change to a larger nib for the main names or write them in a different script. Even the most formal invitation might benefit from a discreet border or small decorative device or illustration.

Designing an invitation for printing means preparing artwork in the form of a pasteup, with calligraphy written in black and with color instructions for the printer. If you are reproducing the invitations by photocopying, they can be copied in black and white or color onto white or colored paper sufficiently thick to cut or fold into cards. Your invitation will usually need to comply to a regular size and shape used by the printer, and, if you work larger, you will have to prepare your artwork to scale (see "Sizing up," p. 48).

The wedding invitation shown here had to give prominence to the names of the bride and the groom, while conveying varying levels of information about the wedding and reception clearly and attractively.

Choosing a script •

Determining the size •

Selecting the format •

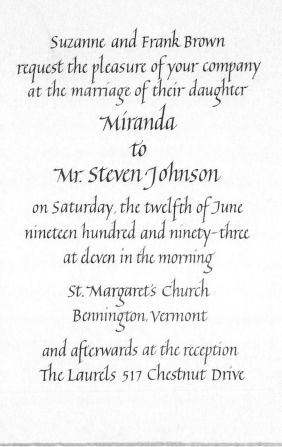

THE PRINTED INVITATION
The invitation is printed on a white card with a silver deckled edge. The result is elegant and restrained.

THUMBNAILS

The first part in the planning process is to sketch out a few layout alternatives from the text supplied. At this stage, it is the format of the invitation and the distribution of the words within that format that are the main concerns. Four options all with centered text are tried. The wide vertical format is selected for development.

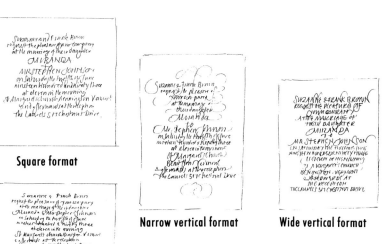

Square format

Narrow vertical format

Wide vertical format

Horizontal format

EXPERIMENTING WITH LETTERFORMS

Italic minuscules and capitals — being both formal and decorative — were the obvious choice for this kind of occasion. The precise details of width and spacing, however, need to be worked out. An all-capitals version and three versions of the minuscules from wide to narrow are tried.

Suzanne and Frank Brown
Standard italic minuscules with capitals

Suzanne and Frank Brown
Narrow italic minuscules with capitals

Suzanne and Frank Brown
Standard italic minuscules with extra spacing

SUZANNE & FRANK BROWN
Italic capitals with slight flourishes

CHOOSING THE PAPER

The choice of paper or card for calligraphic work that is to be printed is subject to considerations that are different from those taken into account when selecting a surface to write on (see pp. 36–37). For printed work you are primarily concerned with color, weight, and texture. Obtain samples from the printer and judge them in relation to the color of ink you are using and the overall effect you are aiming to achieve.

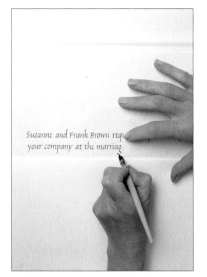 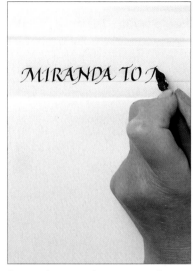 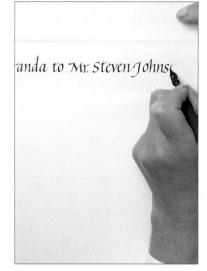

1 *The text is written in the chosen version of italic with a Mitchell's No. 4 nib to 5 nib widths. Writing of this size is designed to be reduced in printing to the dimensions of the finished invitation.*

2 *A preliminary decision is made to render the names of the bridal couple in swash capitals, using a Mitchell's No. 3 nib.*

3 *An alternative version of the names in italic minuscules, also in the larger nib size, is tried for comparison.*

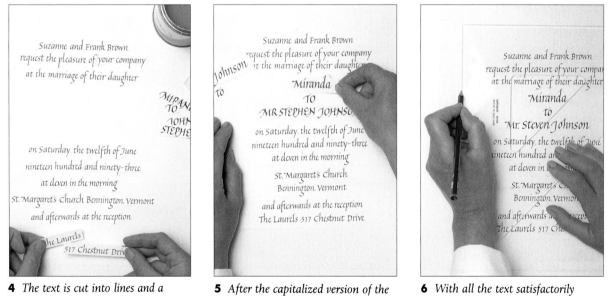

4 *The text is cut into lines and a pasteup is started with spacing assessed by eye. When the arrangement is judged to be right, accurately measured lines can be ruled to guide the final pasteup.*

5 *After the capitalized version of the couple's names is pasted up, it is compared with the minuscule version. The decision is made to substitute the minuscule script.*

6 *With all the text satisfactorily pasted in position, margins are ruled in blue pencil to show the printer the final proportions required. The margins must be in proportion to the size of the final printed invitation.*

Gallery

Calligraphy in invitation design can be used on its own or in harmony with type. Flourishes are a natural choice for calligraphic enhancement of invitations but other decorative elements may also be used to great effect. Sensitivity of design can extend to the choice of paper, the way in which the invitation is folded, and the addressing of the envelope. Creating invitations is an excellent way of putting calligraphy to practical use.

MATCHING INVITATIONS — Angela Hickey

This pair of wedding invitations — one to the wedding, the other to the reception — show the elegant use of flourished italics.

DECORATED INVITATION — Timothy Noad

In this original design for a wedding invitation, simple decorative motifs provide added interest. The text is written in formal italic with emphasis provided by changes of scale.

WEDDING INVITATION — Bonnie Leah

This delicate design is printed on fine quality white paper with an original touch added by the use of Japanese lace paper backing. Folded dimensions: 5¼" × 4" (13.5 cm × 10 cm).

137

Letterhead

PROJECTS

Designing a letterhead is a straightforward and rewarding project for calligraphy beginners. It can also provide interesting design challenges for more advanced calligraphers who have more scripts and decorative techniques at their disposal.

You will need to consider which type of lettering is most appropriate to the person or business whose letterhead you are designing. Do you want the letterhead to look quiet and formal or eye-catching and lively? If the former, a Roman bookhand or formal italic is a good choice. If the latter, a vigorously written cursive italic might be attractive. Relative emphasis within the design can be provided by variations in size, weight, color, and letterform.

A further element you may wish to incorporate is a motif or logo. This could be a simple graphic device or a sophisticated illustration, depending on your skill and the requirements of your client.

The placement of each element in the design in relation to the whole needs to be carefully worked out. Do you want a close vertical texture for impact or wide spacing for elegance? Is the alignment to be to the right, left, centered, or asymmetrical? And how is the letterhead to be placed on the page?

Beyond the design considerations, you also have to plan how the artwork is to be submitted to the printer. A preliminary discussion with the printer to establish the requirements can avoid expensive mistakes.

The letterhead project shown on the following pages is for a ceramics studio. It needed to convey the handcrafted character of a professional business.

Creating an identity •

Planning a logo •

Producing artwork for printing •

THE PRINTED VERSION
Calligraphic lettering provides an original company identity that can be used on a letterhead and a business card.

SELECTING A SCRIPT

The first task is to choose a script that is in keeping with the image the business wants to project. Uncials or half uncials seem good initial choices with their craft-based associations. Various scripts are tried.

The half uncial script with its attractive rounded letterforms, is selected for development.

Serifed uncials at 4½ nib widths

Half uncials at 4 nib widths

Uncials at 3½ nib widths

ALTERNATIVE LAYOUTS

Having decided on a script, the next stage is to work out a layout. The main issues to be determined at this stage are the size of the lettering and its alignment. Rough pencil sketches are adequate for this purpose. It is decided that the name of the business should be rendered in the largest size. The relative size of the rest of the text needs to be worked out. Experiments with a logo are also tried at this stage.

Centered layout, two text sizes

Ragged left-oriented layout, three text sizes

Left-oriented layout with logo, three text sizes

Right-aligned layout, three text sizes

THE FINAL DESIGN

Elements of the second and third layouts (above) have been incorporated into the final design. The text arrangement of the second layout (with slight adjustments to text size) is combined with the logo suggestion of the third. The letterhead is to be centered on the paper.

Ragged left-oriented layout

All lettering in half uncials

Three sizes of text

Pen-drawn logo

the studio.
little haven ceramics
93 MAIN STREET · LITTLE HAVEN · CT 06037

139

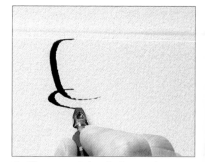

1 *The writing of the large-size lettering is started between lines ruled to 4 nib widths. A Mitchell's No. 0 nib is used, producing lettering that is larger than it will appear in the final printed form. Reduction sharpens the letterforms.*

2 *Because the letterhead is to be printed from a pasteup, small imperfections can be painted out in opaque white. This is a bleed-proof paint that effectively covers any underlying ink.*

3 *The artwork for the logo is drawn using a Mitchell's No. 0 nib. A textured watercolor paper is used, which gives a rough appearance to the work.*

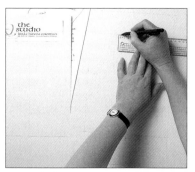

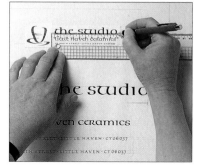

4 *Final adjustments to the layout are made before pasting down the lettering and artwork. Guidelines for the pasteup are ruled up.*

5 *Photocopies of each element — reduced in size where necessary — are pasted carefully in position to show the final effect.*

6 *The intended size of each element is measured from the pasteup and calculated as a percentage of the original so that instructions can be given for a photostatic reduction.*

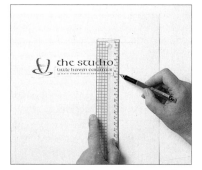

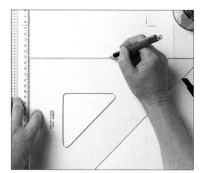

7 *The exact positions of the artwork and lettering are also measured from the pasteup and noted.*

8 *The margins and precise guidelines for the positioning of the letterhead on the paper are marked for a final "camera-ready" pasteup for the printer. Nonreproducible blue pencil, which will not show up in the printing, is used.*

9 *The final pasteup of the artwork and reduced-size photostat of the lettering is completed for printing. Instructions on color and paper type are given to the printer separately.*

Letterheads provide a design challenge. Whether you are commissioned to design a formal and understated image or something eye-catching, the creation of an appropriate image is an excellent design opportunity. The letterheads by skilled calligraphers shown on this page illustrate the interesting possibilities available.

Gallery

BONNIE LEAH LETTERING AND DESIGN

1801 DOVE STREET SUITE 104

NEWPORT BEACH CA 92660

714·752·7820

RIBBON DECORATED LETTERHEAD
Bonnie Leah

This delicate stationery design (above) shows the sensitive combination of decorated calligraphic letterforms and type. The diamond shape and ribbon decoration provide an original touch. Dimensions: 11″ × 8¹/₂″ (28 cm × 22 cm).

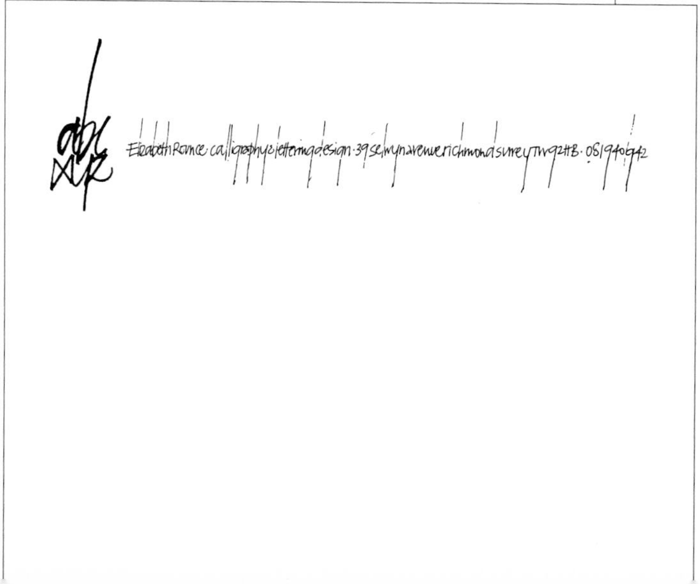

GEORGIA DEAVER

Elizabeth Rounce calligraphy lettering design · 39 selwyn avenue richmond surrey TW9 2HB · 081 940 6742

VERTICAL LETTERHEAD
Christopher Haanes

The combination of lively flourished italic with red type makes for a sophisticated image. Further interest is created by the vertical placement of the calligraphy.

PRINTED LETTERHEADS
Georgia Deaver (above left) and Elizabeth Rounce (below left)

These examples show how careful attention to contrasts of weight and scale can provide great impact.

Poetry broadsheet

5 PROJECTS

A broadsheet is a single sheet of paper containing one or more poems, sections of a poem, or pieces of prose that are linked by theme and can be read across the sheet, with no need to turn pages. A broadsheet design should not be too complicated, or it may detract from the meaning of the text and appear contrived. A simple approach is usually the key to success.

The broadsheet is a good project for the inexperienced calligrapher, and one to which you can return as you progress, because it offers plenty of opportunity for practicing newly acquired skills and using them creatively. Working on texts and themes helps you release and develop your imagination and find ways of interpreting your personal reactions to the passages you choose to write. This can be a stimulating experience and a source of fun. A finished broadsheet can be framed and displayed. The choice of quotations is crucial, because a personal interest in the theme will give the work excitement and a sense of discovery. If you enjoy the time spent on the project, this will communicate itself to the viewer.

In the broadsheet shown here, texts were "hung" around a central piece of writing. The calligrapher was fascinated by the sense of wildness and the closeness with nature reflected in some early Irish poems. The core text was powerful and deeply imaginative, and the additional quotations enhanced this feeling while also creating atmosphere. The theme linked the contrasts of beauty and harshness in a landscape integrally bound up with the lives of its inhabitant birds and animals. The scripts were chosen to create an interplay between the central and the surrounding texts, while harmonious colors, repeated shapes and images, and gentle contrasts served to unify the design.

Arranging text elements •

Harmonizing script and illustration •

Displaying the finished piece •

THE FINISHED WORK
The completed panel shows a delicate harmony of text and illustration. To display the work a natural limed-wood frame is selected, whose muted color does not overwhelm the subtle colors of the lettering.

THE EVOLVING IDEA

The initial design ideas for both the text and the illustration in this project are developed simultaneously. The calligrapher sketches broad areas to represent the component elements, so that the final design will form a unified whole.

The design is a triptych with the main text placed centrally and the two subsidiary texts on either side. At this stage, the calligrapher's notes indicate that she plans for the focus of the piece to be reinforced by rendering the main text in a darker tone than the subsidiary texts — a decision that is later partially reversed.

Thumbnail sketches with accompanying notes show the development of the illustration ideas.

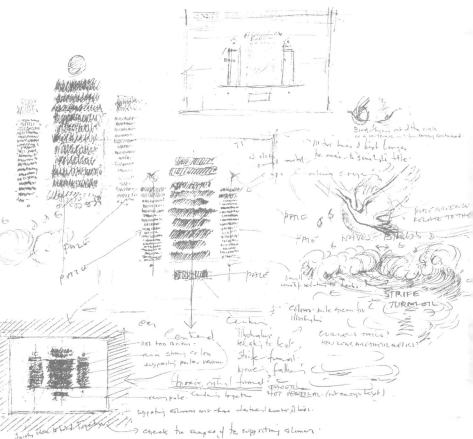

THE FINAL ROUGH

The calligrapher refines her ideas in a rough layout in which she determines the positions of the three component poems and the illustration areas. The text is rendered in italic script and in colors approximating those to be used in the finished piece in order to make the rough as accurate as possible.

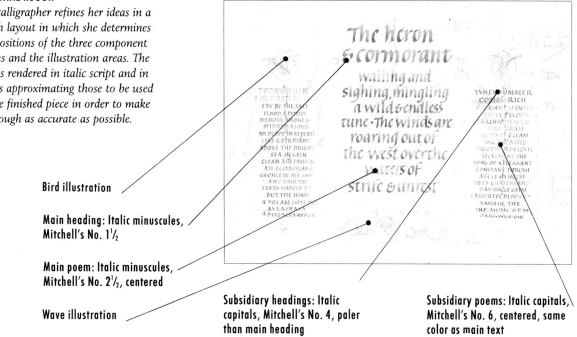

Bird illustration

Main heading: Italic minuscules, Mitchell's No. 1½

Main poem: Italic minuscules, Mitchell's No. 2½, centered

Wave illustration

Subsidiary headings: Italic capitals, Mitchell's No. 4, paler than main heading

Subsidiary poems: Italic capitals, Mitchell's No. 6, centered, same color as main text

143

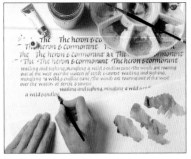

1 *The initial writing of the text uses the selected colors in order to judge their effect. Different colors are tried on scraps of paper first.*

2 *Photocopies of the text are cut out and pasted in position. The central panel is placed first. Care is taken to ensure that the panels are evenly balanced with equal numbers of lines. Several attempts are needed.*

3 *With all elements placed in position, measurements of the line spacing are taken from the pasteup to be transferred to the final version.*

4 *Further work is needed on the illustrations. The calligrapher experiments with different color treatments before making a final decision. Here a muted yellow wash is painted over a pencil drawing.*

5 *The final writing is started. The central panel is completed first, because its position determines the placement of the other elements.*

6 *Using the pasteup as a guide, ruled lines to mark the position of the side panels are drawn in relation to the central panel.*

7 *The side panels are written along the ruled guidelines.*

8 *The illustrations are the last element to be added. They are carefully drawn in pencil before the colored washes are put in.*

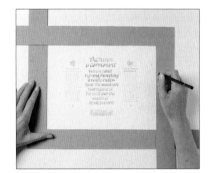

9 *A final decision on margins is made after the work is completed. L-shaped cards are used to judge the margins, and these are penciled in. The broadsheet is later trimmed, and a mat is added for display.*

Most of the panels of poetry shown in this gallery are examples of personal responses to the text expressed in calligraphic terms. For calligraphers at all levels, poetry and literature in general can serve as a major stimulus for experimental creative work. Working from soundly understood letterforms, you can use poetry to explore variations in weight, slope, and layout. Color, too, can be brought into play as a means of expressing the mood of the poem, bright and energetic to quietly harmonious — the choice belongs to the calligrapher.

Gallery

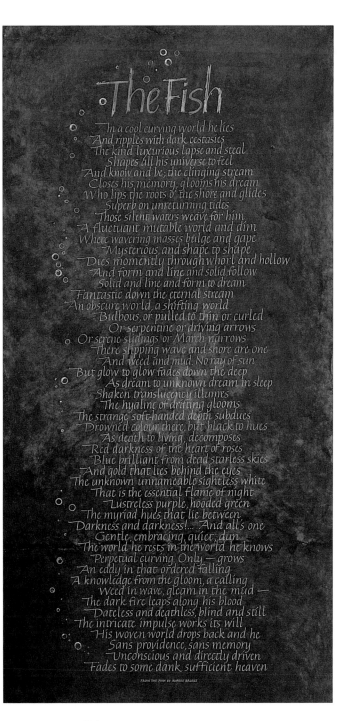

IN THE HIGHLANDS — Louise Donaldson

This calligraphic panel based on a poem by Robert Louis Stevenson uses contrasting styles and sizes of lettering. Dimensions: 16½″ × 26″ (40.5 × 64 cm).

THE FISH — Janet Mehigan

Written in gouache in a lightweight italic script, this rendering of a poem by Rupert Brooke is an example of the effectiveness of a simple layout. Dimensions: 19″ × 40″ (47 cm × 98 cm).

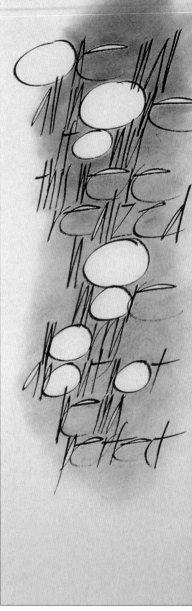

CROSSROADS – Nancy R. Leavitt

This imaginative interpretation (above) of a text by Karl Young uses a close-knit vertical texture of different-size versals. Color changes set off the lettering from the background, which links the various elements of the design. Dimensions: 14" × 8¾" (36 cm × 22 cm).

JAVEL – Julia Vance

The use of heavyweight dancing capitals with close interline spacing (above) creates a lively graphic effect. The small gilded capitals provide an interesting contrast within the design. Dimensions: 20" × 24" (51 cm × 61 cm).

ONE IN ALL, ALL IN ONE – Paivi Vesanto

The compressed slanting letters of this italic-based script (above) give a strong diagonal emphasis to the design. The exaggerated open letters left uncolored on a Conté crayon background, produce an interesting change of texture. Dimensions: 9" × 27" (23 cm × 69 cm).

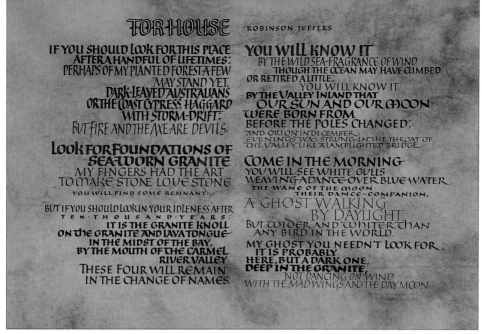

TOR HOUSE

ROBINSON JEFFERS

IF YOU SHOULD LOOK FOR THIS PLACE
AFTER A HANDFUL OF LIFETIMES:
PERHAPS OF MY PLANTED FOREST A FEW
MAY STAND YET,
DARK-LEAVED AUSTRALIANS
OR THE COAST CYPRESS HAGGARD
WITH STORM-DRIFT;
BUT FIRE AND THE AXE ARE DEVILS.

LOOK FOR FOUNDATIONS OF
SEA-WORN GRANITE
MY FINGERS HAD THE ART
TO MAKE STONE LOVE STONE
YOU WILL FIND SOME REMNANT.

BUT IF YOU SHOULD LOOK IN YOUR IDLENESS AFTER
TEN·THOUSAND·YEARS;
IT IS THE GRANITE KNOLL
ON THE GRANITE AND LAVA TONGUE
IN THE MIDST OF THE BAY,
BY THE MOUTH OF THE CARMEL
RIVER VALLEY
THESE FOUR WILL REMAIN
IN THE CHANGE OF NAMES.

YOU WILL KNOW IT
BY THE WILD SEA-FRAGRANCE OF WIND
THOUGH THE OCEAN MAY HAVE CLIMBED
OR RETIRED A LITTLE;
YOU WILL KNOW IT
BY THE VALLEY INLAND THAT
OUR SUN AND OUR MOON
WERE BORN FROM
BEFORE THE POLES CHANGED;
AND ORION IN DECEMBER
EVENINGS WAS STRUNG IN THE THROAT OF
THE VALLEY LIKE A LAMPLIGHTED BRIDGE

COME IN THE MORNING
YOU WILL SEE WHITE GULLS
WEAVING A DANCE OVER BLUE WATER
THE WANE OF THE MOON
THEIR DANCE-COMPANION,
A GHOST WALKING
BY DAYLIGHT,
BUT WILDER AND WHITER THAN
ANY BIRD IN THE WORLD.
MY GHOST YOU NEEDN'T LOOK FOR;
IT IS PROBABLY
HERE, BUT A DARK ONE,
DEEP IN THE GRANITE,
NOT DANCING ON WIND
WITH THE MAD WINGS AND THE DAY MOON

TOR HOUSE – Sheila Waters

A wide range of capitals is used in this interpretation of a poem by Robinson Jeffers (above). Changes in weight, size, and compression provide subtle variations in emphasis. The delicate color of the vellum gently unites the text areas. Dimensions: 23" × 15½" (58 × 39 cm).

RIDDLE

I STRETCH BEYOND THE BOUNDS OF THE WORLD,
I'M SMALLER THAN A WORM,
OUTSTRIP THE SUN,
I SHINE MORE BRIGHTLY THAN THE MOON,
THE SWELLING SEAS
THE FAIR FACE OF THE EARTH
AND ALL THE GREEN FIELDS
ARE WITHIN MY CLASP, I COVER THE DEPTHS
AND PLUNGE BENEATH HELL,
I ASCEND ABOVE HEAVEN
HIGHLAND OF RENOWN, I REACH BEYOND
THE BOUNDARIES
OF THE LAND OF BLESSED ANGELS,
I FILL FAR AND WIDE THE CORNERS OF THE EARTH
AND THE OCEAN STREAMS

SAY WHAT MY NAME IS

FROM THE EXETER BOOK OF RIDDLES TRANSLATED BY KEVIN CROSSLEY-HOLLAND

CREATION – Gillian Hazeldine

This text from the Exeter Book of Riddles (left) is rendered in heavyweight capitals with a scattering of lightweight Roman capitals, creating an interesting overall texture. The asymmetrical layout adds to the sense of movement. The gouache lettering is enlivened by the use of small areas of gold. Dimensions: 17¾" × 12" (45 cm × 30 cm).

Poster

PROJECTS

Calligraphy can be a striking alternative or complement to print in poster design. A calligraphic poster is an ideal challenge whatever your level of skill, giving you the chance to put your writing and design abilities to specific practical use. Whatever its specific aim, the successful poster should catch the eye of the intended audience and present the essential information clearly, so that it can be read "on the run."

A poster can be reproduced at low cost and look attractive, even if it has to be in a single color. Designing for one color can stimulate imaginative use of both contrasts created by the lettering itself and of the space in and around the text. Color can be introduced, if needed, by using colored paper or adding a splash of color by hand to each poster.

Some posters suffer from "overload," with too much happening and no focus; others are simply dull. You can use lettering alone to create an eye-catching focus or choose suitable imagery to fulfill this role. It is important to create an atmosphere in the poster that is suitable to the subject by wise choice of styles and sizes of lettering, and by considered use of space and illustration (if needed). Whether you are creating a notice for a classical concert or an announcement for a contemporary dance performance, all the design elements must be carefully selected and balanced.

In posters, as in all design, there are no absolute rules, but experience provides helpful hints. The poster shown here is a low-budget design for a jazz concert to be printed in black on a photocopier. The poster needs to suggest a dynamic but controlled atmosphere while conveying a clear and eye-catching message.

Producing a design that works well in two colors •

Organizing the information into an eye-catching, easy-to-read form •

PRINTED POSTERS
The finished calligraphic artwork is printed onto different colored papers. The green paper is selected for the final print-run.

ASSESSING THE TEXT

In most cases the client supplies the text for the poster, as in this case, in the form of typed copy. The first task is to organize the information into "bite size" pieces and sort them according to their relative importance. Here, the calligrapher also suggests ways of making the wording punchier.

10 YEARS

TENTH ANNIVERSARY OF JAZZ AT THE WAREHOUSE

SPECIAL FREE CONCERT (WITH) ROY LEWIS BAND

(ON) THURSDAY 18th MAY (AT) 8pm (AT) THE WAREHOUSE

RIVERSIDE SELBY (NOTE:) FACILITIES FOR

WHEELCHAIR ACCESS

WHEELCHAIRS (AND) BAR

THUMBNAIL SKETCHES

Various layout ideas are tried, incorporating different sizes and styles of lettering. The word "JAZZ" is picked out to provide the main focus.

Horizontal orientation, upturned lettering at left margin

Focus in lower half of design with diagonal subsidiary elements

Focus in upper half, aligned left

Focus in upper half, aligned left to solid band in margin

Focus in upper half, solid bands at top and bottom, aligned left

Focus in upper half, main lettering breaking into band in left margin

THE FINAL DESIGN

The final thumbnail (above) provides the best combination of elements, with the broken black band providing contrast and emphasis, leading the eye down the poster to the subsidiary information. In this final rough (right), the addition of horizontal lines above and below the word "JAZZ" strengthens the focus. At this time decisions on letterform, weight, and size are firmed up. All the lettering is in compressed italic, which conveys an appropriate sense of controlled energy. Variations in size and weight provide different levels of emphasis.

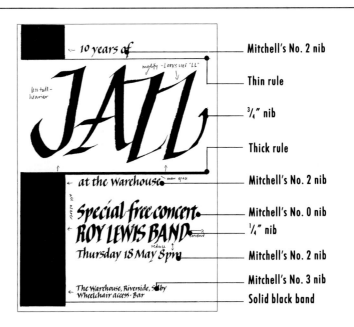

← 10 years of —————— Mitchell's No. 2 nib

mighty - LOOKS LIKE "LL"

less tall – heavier

Thin rule

¾" nib

Thick rule

← at the Warehouse Mitchell's No. 2 nib

Special free concert Mitchell's No. 0 nib

ROY LEWIS BAND ¼" nib

Thursday 18 May 8pm Mitchell's No. 2 nib

The Warehouse, Riverside, Selby Mitchell's No. 3 nib
Wheelchair access · Bar Solid black band

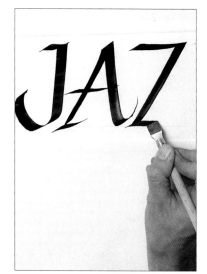

1 *The text is written out in preparation for a preliminary pasteup. At this point it is still possible to fine-tune the size and weight of the lettering. Here the main word is written using a ¹/₂″ (12 mm) plain-stroke pen.*

2 *A pasteup is completed using photocopies of the lettering. "JAZZ" has been rewritten using a ³/₄″ (20 mm) nib. At this stage, fine adjustments of text position are made.*

3 *Measurements of line spacing are taken from the rough pasteup and transferred to the final (camera-ready) pasteup.*

4 *The text is placed in its final position on the final pasteup.*

5 *The black bands and rules are carefully drawn in with indelible felt-tip pens. Any marks and imperfections — including the edges of the pasted-up text — are covered using correction fluid (or opaque white paint).*

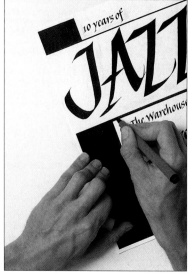

6 *A fine marker pen is used to fill any unevenness in the rules and to ensure the black areas are "solid." The poster is now ready for reproduction. At this stage the choice to print on white or on colored paper is made.*

Gallery

Calligraphic lettering used in poster design can create a visual impact quite different from that which can be achieved with type alone. Key words can be rendered in a style that is specifically designed to be in harmony with the overall message. Extra-broad plain-stroke or multiline pens can be used to great effect in a design where one eye-catching word or image is required. This is also an area where you can adapt the letterforms or create new forms of your own, if this seems appropriate. With posters, the freshness of the image is the key consideration.

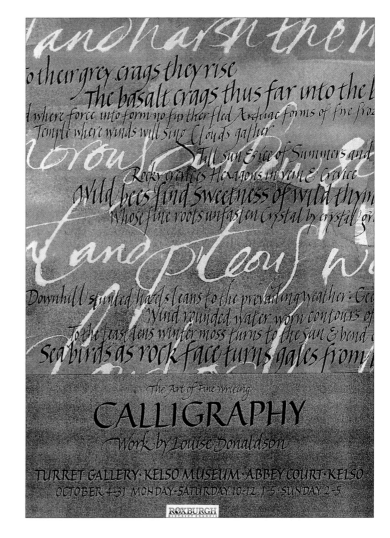

EXHIBITION POSTER — Louise Donaldson

This piece of work (above), uses ruling pen with masking fluid lettering under a gradated wash alongside broad-nib pen calligraphy. Dimensions: $16^{1}/_{2}"$ × 26" (40.5 cm × 66 cm).

TUSCANY — Jenny Kavarana

The diagonal lines of text, bold capitals, strong colors, and a dark background (left) all contribute to the image. The small white lettering makes a pleasing contrast and is united with the rest of the design by the ruled red lines. Dimensions: 24" × 17" (61 cm × 43 cm).

CREATIVE STUDIES — Jenny Kavarana

This exhibition poster (above) uses bold white lettering based on Rudolf Koch's "Neuland" alphabet with a dark background. Close interline spacing and subtle use of color between the letters makes for a striking design. Dimensions: 24" × 17" (61 cm × 43 cm).

151

Concertina book

PROJECTS

This type of simple folded book, which is also a display panel, is a popular application for calligraphy. It combines the opportunity to use a relatively long text at a convenient size, with the challenge of having to design pages that work well when fully opened as well as individually. The need for the design to flow horizontally through the book provides interesting possibilities for both the calligraphy and the illustration. Color can often provide a unifying element through the book.

The concertina book shown here makes use of an anonymous medieval poem about the seasons. The simplicity of the words seems to lend itself well to this intimate treatment, and the continuous nature of a concertina book works well with the idea of the seasonal cycle. The illustration motifs come from medieval symbols for the seasons.

Enhancing text through layout ●

Making a closing cover ●

Using stencil illustration ●

THE FINISHED BOOK
This horizontal format book folds neatly into its cover. Because the cover is fixed only at the front, the book can be opened and extended to show all its pages in a single view.

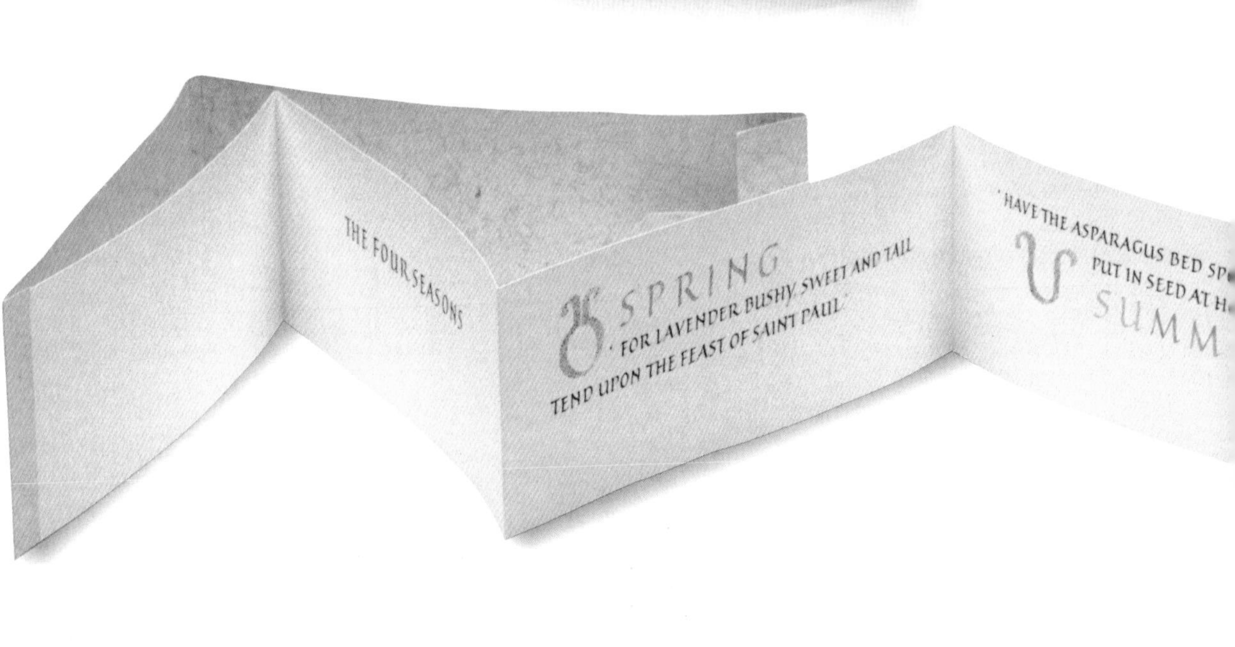

INITIAL LAYOUTS

The decision has already been made to use a horizontal format with illustrations based on the medieval symbols for the seasons. However, the size of the lettering, the relationship of the headings to the text, and the position and treatment of the motif need to be worked out in more detail.

Various rough layouts are tried. The position of the motif at the left of the page remains constant as does the rendering of the text in italic capitals. The major questions to be resolved are the size, weight, and spacing of the text. The rough layouts shown at right show the evolution of the idea, although none of these solutions is eventually selected for development. The idea of widely spaced lettering for the heading proves too weak, and a more conventional letterspacing is adopted.

1 *The text is written and pasted up with the pen-drawn symbol. The verse is written with a Mitchell's No. 4 nib and the heading with a No. 2½. At this stage the final decision on the letterspacing of the heading is made.*

2 *The final pasteup shows the arrangement of the symbol, heading, and verse on the page. A pasteup is needed for each page.*

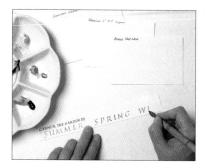

3 *Final choices of paper and color are made. The project requires a paper that is suitable for both ink and watercolor. A pale cream textured paper is chosen after testing the selected colors on it.*

4 *The motifs are to be stenciled. The first stage is to trace each pen-drawn motif in pencil.*

5 *A piece of low-tack masking film is adhered over the tracing.*

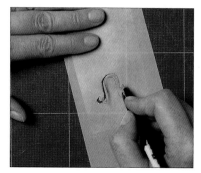

6 *A craft knife is used to cut out the traced symbol, accurately following the drawn outlines.*

7 *The masking film is carefully peeled away from the tracing paper and placed so that the symbol is in its final position on the paper. The surrounding paper is carefully masked. The chosen colors are mixed and spattered over the stencil using a stencil brush.*

8 *The text is written on the pages in black ink in the positions specified by the final pasteup.*

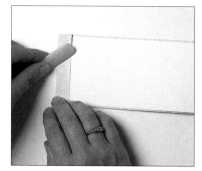

9 *The cover is cut to allow ⅛" (3 mm) extra at the top and bottom plus ½" (13 mm) at the front and a 1" (25 mm) flap with 2" (50 mm) tab at the back (see p. 152). The folds of the cover are scored (see also p. 159). The front flap is glued to the first page only.*

The different concertina books illustrated on this page indicate the wide scope open to you in designing a concertina book. As the examples show, this type of book is an attractive and manageable project for a calligraphy beginner.

LOVE – Mary Noble

This unusual book (above) consists of two concertina sheets with slits that are slotted together vertically. Dimensions (opened): 10" × 25" (25.5 cm × 64 cm).

ANGLO SAXON RIDDLE – Anne Irwin

The well-planned simplicity of this concertina book (left) is the key to its success. Rubber stamp motifs are used alongside text written in a basic Roman bookhand. Dimensions (opened): 3" × 108" (7.5 cm × 275 cm).

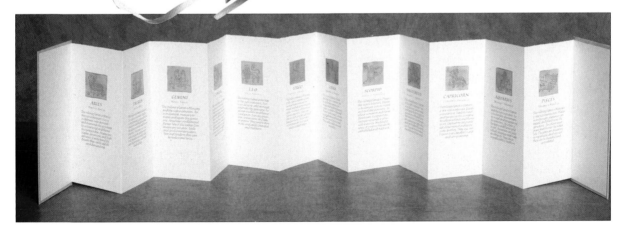

ZODIAC – Patricia Lovett

This attractive concertina book (above) based on the signs of the zodiac incorporates subtle illustrations over painted background squares. Dimensions: 5" × 8" (12.5 cm × 20.5 cm).

Manuscript book

PROJECTS

Books were handwritten from Roman times until the Renaissance, and even after the invention of printing, rich patrons still commissioned manuscript volumes. The manuscript book continues to offer useful design experience to calligraphers at all levels, posing questions about the relationship between text area and margins, page size and shape, length of writing line, size, weight and styles of writing, and the choice of writing and binding materials.

Even the beginner can make an attractive manuscript book, because the book lends itself just as well to the straightforward treatment of a short text as to longer and more elaborate writing and designs. Books can have one or many sections, and illustration can range from a simple decorative element, such as a symbol, to ornate illumination. A single section is best for a first book. Traditionally this consists of 16 pages — including a title page and several blank pages at the beginning and end of the book, so that there are about five to seven pages of writing — but there can be fewer if you prefer. You can include a discreet colophon at the back of the book, giving your name and the date of writing. You can then sew on a simple cover with or without decoration.

Any page proportion is possible, and your eye is the final arbiter. However, handwritten books usually look most effective with more generous margins than we are used to seeing in printed books.

The text selected for this manuscript book is a short and lighthearted essay by an Irish writer, John B. Keane, taken from his collection *Strong Tea.*

Planning margins •

Using decorative capitals •

Sewing a cover •

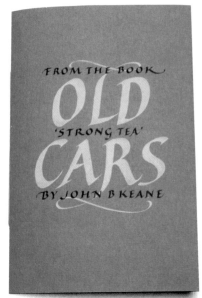

THE FINISHED BOOK
The cover, with its simple, but decorative lettering (left), harmonizes with the straightforward calligraphy of the inside pages (below).

DETERMINING FORMAT AND PAGE SIZE

After reading the text and getting a feeling for its overall character, jot down some preliminary layout ideas. At this stage you should consider format, page size, and first thoughts on the script to be used. It is also important to work with double-page spreads.

The thumbnail sketches shown at right indicate some of the options tried for this project. After reviewing these possibilities, the calligrapher decides to pursue a relatively wide vertical format.

Large capitals start, left-aligned text

Narrow vertical format

Centered capital start

Drop capital start

Spaced capital start

Wider vertical format

Horizontal format

WORKING OUT THE LETTERFORMS

Having decided on the format, it is possible to work out the treatment of the text in more detail. Although the text is humorous, it is decided not to overemphasize this by using a zany script. A plain italic has the right feeling of simplicity. However, to give texture to the page and to provide variation in pace, larger colored capitals are chosen for the paragraph openings. Experiments for these are shown at right.

WORKING OUT MARGINS

The margins of a manuscript book are calculated in a different way from those of a calligraphic panel. As a beginner you should follow the standard formula that produces margins in which the outer margin is twice the inner one and the bottom margin is twice the top margin.

1 *Draw an accurate double-page layout to your chosen page size.*

2 *Draw diagonals between points A, B, C, and D as shown.*

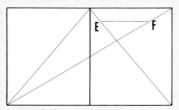

3 *Mark the top margin with a horizontal between E and F.*

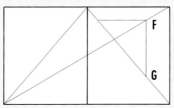

4 *Rule in the right margin with a rightangle from F to G.*

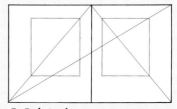

5 *Rule in the remaining margins. The left-hand page mirrors the right.*

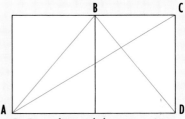

157

1 *Using a Mitchell's No. 4 nib and black watercolor, the calligrapher writes out the text for a rough pasteup.*

2 *Various styles — italic and versal — of introductory capitals are tried at different sizes. The calligrapher decides to use versals.*

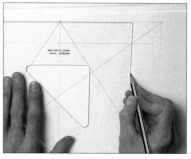

3 *Margins are ruled on a sheet of paper for the pasteup.*

4 *Lines that will act as guides for the pasteup are ruled, based on preliminary decisions made when selecting the letterform.*

5 *The written text is cut out and pasted in position on the writing lines. Tweezers are useful for picking up and positioning small pieces of text.*

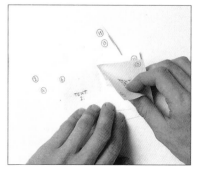

6 *A manuscript book is made up of sheets folded in half — each comprising four pages of the book. These are called folios. It is a good idea to prepare a miniature book that allows you to check and number the pages.*

7 *After all decisions on layout and pagination have been made, the next stage is the final writing. With the versal capital penciled in, the small black lettering is written first.*

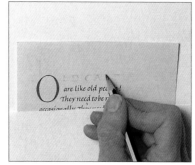

8 *The versal capital is completed next in blue gouache, and the introduction in small capitals is penciled in.*

9 *The small capitals are written in pen in the same blue gouache.*

MAKING A COVER

A manuscript book needs a well-made cover to protect the inner pages. It should be made from heavy paper that will withstand handling. Once you trim and fold (see right) the cover, sew it to the text pages as shown below.

FOLDING THE COVER

The cover should be larger than the page dimensions; allow about $1/4" - 1/2"$ (6 mm–12 mm) extra at the top, bottom, and outside edges. Give the cover generous flaps of about two-thirds the cover width. Once the cover is cut, score the inside folds of the spine and flaps using a pointed, but not sharp tool, such as the ends of a closed pair of scissors.

SEWING THE COVER

Carefully position the folded folios inside the cover. Pierce stitch holes from the inside fold of the center folio through the outside spine fold of the cover. Using heavyweight thread and a strong needle, pass the needle through the middle hole in the inside fold in the center folio, leaving a long loose end as shown in the diagram. Continue to sew following the sequence illustrated. Be careful not to divide the thread as you pass through a hole for the second time. To finish, tie the two loose ends together inside the book and trim.

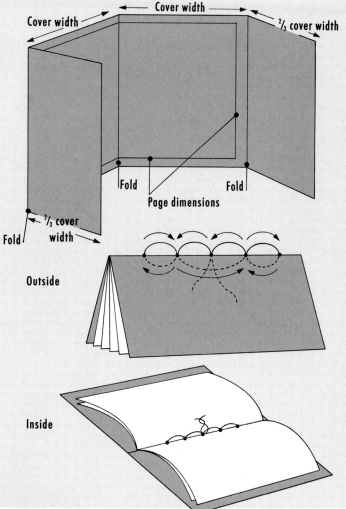

Cover width Cover width $2/3$ cover width

Fold   Fold

Page dimensions

Fold $2/3$ cover width

Outside

Inside

10 After the writing is complete, the pages are trimmed (if necessary) and assembled in the correct order. The book is then placed on the chosen cover paper, and the dimensions of the cover are measured and marked.

11 The trimmed cover and book are sewn together with strong thread (see above).

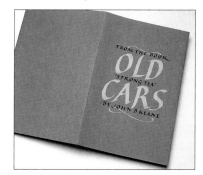

12 The finished book has a calligraphic cover that echoes the treatment of the inside pages.

This selection of manuscript books illustrates a rich variety of approaches. It shows how a well-written classical format has great serenity and elegance, while a more experimental approach to the text has different strengths — most importantly, stimulating the interplay of movement and stillness. This selection also demonstrates that beautifully written lettering has its own decorative quality, but that illustration sensitively blended with the text can enhance the overall design. Whether you choose a simple or complex design, making a manuscript book is a feasible project for calligraphers at every stage of learning. It is an intimate design vehicle for a thoughtful and personal approach.

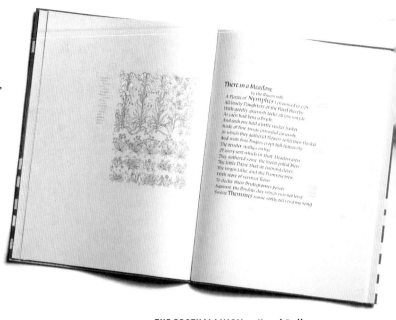

THE PROTHALAMION — Hazel Dolby

This spread combines gray gouache text and watercolor illustration. The generous margins enhance the delicacy of the whole. Dimensions: $13^{1}/_{2}$" × 10" (34 cm × 25 cm).

I take the word and go over it
as though it were nothing more than human shape
its arrangements awe me and I find my way
through each variation in the spoken word —
I utter and I am and without speaking I approach
the limit of words and the silence.

the pure wine
of language
inexhaustible
water

I drink to the word, raising
a word or a shining cup,
in it I drink
the pure wine of language
or inexhaustable water,
maternal source of words,
and cup and water and wine
give rise to my song.

THE WORD — Kate Ridyard

In this book, the freely written italic-based script done in red gouache with a ruling pen contrasts strikingly with the black edged-pen italic. Dimensions (spread): 12" × $4^{1}/_{2}$" (30.5 cm × 11.5 cm).

MONTAGNA-ACQUA — Monica Dengo

This title page from a book of the writings of François Cheng shows an interesting design created by contrasting formal italic broad-pen capitals with a lively italic written with a ruling pen. Both ink and gouache are used. Dimensions: 7⅛″ × 10⅝″ (20 cm × 26 cm).

SPEAK TO THE EARTH — Suzanne Moore

This centerfold shows an unusual and sensitive presentation of a double-page spread. The close vertical texture of capitals balances and harmonizes with the illuminated symbol on the facing page, and the delicate flourishes on both pages further unite the spread. Dimensions (closed size): 16½″ × 10½″ (42 cm × 27 cm).

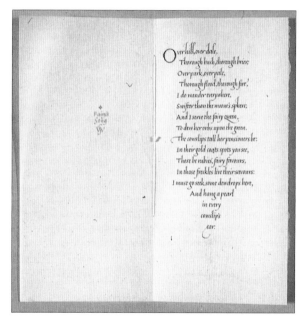

FAIRY'S SONG — Joan Pilsbury

This elegant double-page spread of a Shakespearean text written on vellum in formal italic shows the timeless quality of a well-written italic. The initial O is raised and burnished gold. The generous space around the text enhances the calm quality of the whole. Dimensions: 10″ × 9¼″ (25 cm × 24.5 cm).

Decorative border

PROJECTS

5

Although good calligraphy should be able to stand alone, there are situations in formal or creative work where decoration can enhance a text. Decorative borders from Eastern and Western historical manuscripts are an infinitely varied source of reference for contemporary calligraphy. These borders may influence your own designs, but try to use them in new and creative ways.

The wealth of designs in Western manuscripts include simple colored linear borders, sometimes consisting of differently colored bands of varying widths. These may be plain, or divided into decorated rectangles, or feature repeating patterns of geometric or intertwined plant elements. Sometimes the border is an extension of a decorated initial letter. A myriad of plant designs, including complex floral designs, are found in Flemish, French, and Italian manuscripts from the late medieval period onward.

Possibilities for contemporary borders abound. Apart from plants and geometric shapes, patterns and symbols from different cultures or religions can be a source of ideas. Whatever the design, small illustrations can be introduced at intervals, perhaps enclosed in circles or other shapes.

As with any other form of decoration, the border must be appropriate to the subject and script, and form an integral part of the work as a whole. Plant borders may be contained by colored or gilded lines of suitable width, or left with the plants themselves forming the outer edges of the design.

The floral border in this project is suitable for use in a manuscript book or, as shown here, in a framed panel. The text, with its references to nature, seemed to demand such a treatment.

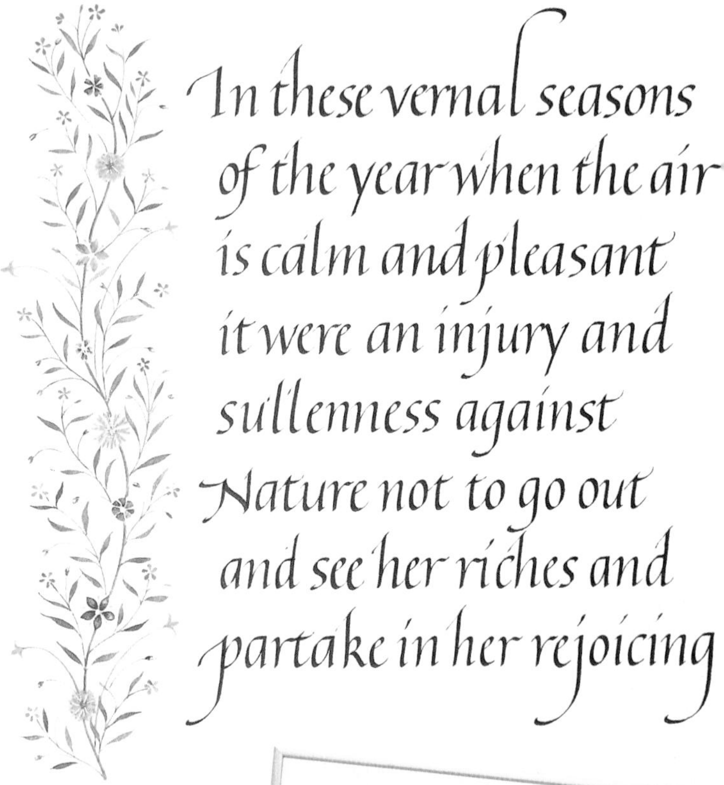

Designing simple illustration •

Balancing text and border •

Using color effectively •

In these vernal seasons of the year when the air is calm and pleasant it were an injury and sullenness against Nature not to go out and see her riches and partake in her rejoicing

THE FINISHED WORK
The delicate floral border together with the elegant italic text would be overwhelmed by a heavy frame and mount. A fine gold frame discreetly complements the calligraphy and decoration.

FIRST THOUGHTS

For this project the first step is to decide on the page format and on the placement of the borders.

Various options shown below are sketched as thumbnails. The final design is vertical with a single border along the left margin (far right).

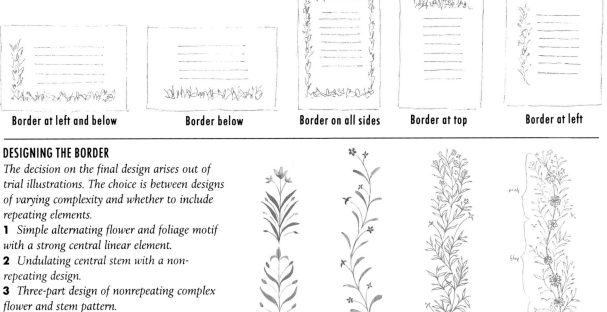

Border at left and below　　**Border below**　　**Border on all sides**　　**Border at top**　　**Border at left**

DESIGNING THE BORDER

The decision on the final design arises out of trial illustrations. The choice is between designs of varying complexity and whether to include repeating elements.

1 *Simple alternating flower and foliage motif with a strong central linear element.*

2 *Undulating central stem with a non-repeating design.*

3 *Three-part design of nonrepeating complex flower and stem pattern.*

4 *Complex flower and stem pattern with strong central emphasis. Repeating color combinations.*

1　　**2**　　**3**　　**4**

THE FINAL DESIGN

In the final layout, shown here as a rough pasteup, the border design shown in example 3 (above) is selected for development. The decision is made to use italics for the text with simple flourishes at selected points to break up the outline. The colors used are clear and bright, but not so strong as to overwhelm the text.

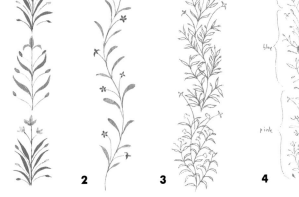

In these vernal seasons of the year when the air is calm and pleasant it were an injury and sullenness against Nature not to go out and see her riches and partake in her rejoicing

Italic text with selective flourishing using a Mitchell's No. 3 nib

Aligned left layout

Border along left margin only

Dense floral design with repeating color combinations

1 *The text is written for a final pasteup using a Mitchell's No. 3 nib.*

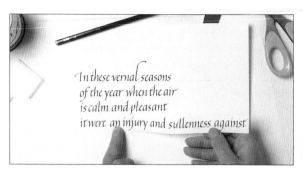

2 *The text is pasted up line by line. Each line is cut to length only when the line length is established.*

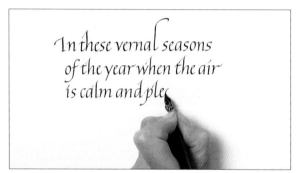

3 *The final writing out of the text follows the pasteup. A heavy, hot-pressed paper is used.*

4 *A tracing is made of the chosen design for the floral border. Placing a pad of paper under the drawing helps you to obtain a good-quality line.*

5 *The traced design is transferred to its final position on the writing sheet by placing graphite paper between the tracing paper and the paper. Simply draw over the tracing, pressing firmly. Any unwanted marks can be removed from the paper with an eraser.*

6 *The final illustration is colored by applying watercolor with a fine brush.*

Decorative borders have been a particularly attractive enhancement of calligraphic work for many centuries in both East and West. Whether realistic, stylized, or invented, floral borders are particularly suited to flowing calligraphic forms. In Western manuscripts, such as a Renaissance Book of Hours, the detail of the painting and gilding is superb. In a simpler form, this kind of illustration is readily accessible to the calligraphy beginner. Whether you are creating a manuscript book or a panel of calligraphy, you will find it rewarding to combine border design with calligraphy.

CALLIGRAPHIC PANEL
Carina Westling

This panel of flowing cursive italic is enhanced by finely painted and gilded borders using an interlaced design. The unusual decision to use two contrasting L-shapes creates an effective balance in conjunction with the circular focal decoration.

DRAPERS' COMPANY 500th ANNIVERSARY CHARTER
Joan Pilsbury and Wendy Westover

This charter, written on vellum in italic with raised and burnished gold versal capitals, is a superb example of a formal document. The beautifully detailed watercolor and gouache borders use plant designs and heraldic elements with gold details. Dimensions: 66" × 54" (168 cm × 137 cm).

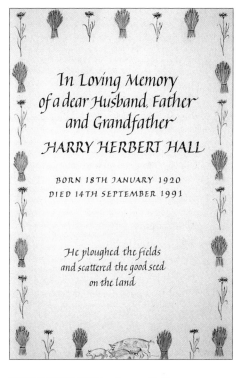

REMEMBRANCE BOOK — Gaynor Goffe

This alternating repeat border painted in gouache is one of a series in a book of remembrance. The border elements of this page are designed to reflect the life of the deceased. Dimensions: 10" × 7" (25 cm × 18 cm).

Illuminated letter

PROJECTS

Illuminated or decorative letters have been employed by calligraphers since medieval times to "lighten" pages of text. In addition to this traditional application of decorative letterwork, designs based on a single letterform can also be used for greeting cards, letterheads, and commemorative panels.

Illuminated letters can encompass a vast array of different types of design, from the fantastic illustrated compositions of medieval manuscripts, through intricate scrollwork, to the colorful modern graphic treatments of this century. What all the best illuminated letters have in common is a harmony between the letterform and the decorative treatment.

You do not have to be an expert illustrator to try your hand at decorative lettering. You can start by copying ideas from early manuscripts (try to find a book of reproductions from a library or museum) and adapting them to your own requirements — using your own color choices, for example. Later, try adding illustration ideas of your own. Simple plant forms are a great source of inspiration.

Versal letterforms were the traditional vehicle for medieval illumination; their built-up forms are ideal for the addition of color or gilding. However, almost any script can be used in a modern context.

In the project shown on the following pages a single letter was decorated using gouache and gilding. The intention was to produce a design for a greeting card.

Adapting a letterform •

Designing decoration •

Applying gold leaf •

FINISHED CARD
The completed letter (above) is mounted on green card from which a "window" has been cut. A greeting could be written on the plain paper fixed inside the card.

PLANNING THE ILLUSTRATION

The design is to be based on the letter Q using a form of versal script known as Lombardic. The letterform, with its spacious counter and graceful tail, provides ample opportunities for decoration within and around the letter. The scrolling form of the tail, in particular, provides a starting point for a design based on curling tendrils of vine leaves. A number of annotated sketches explore the possibilities for this type of design. A major decision is how far to extend the decoration beyond the boundaries of the letterform.

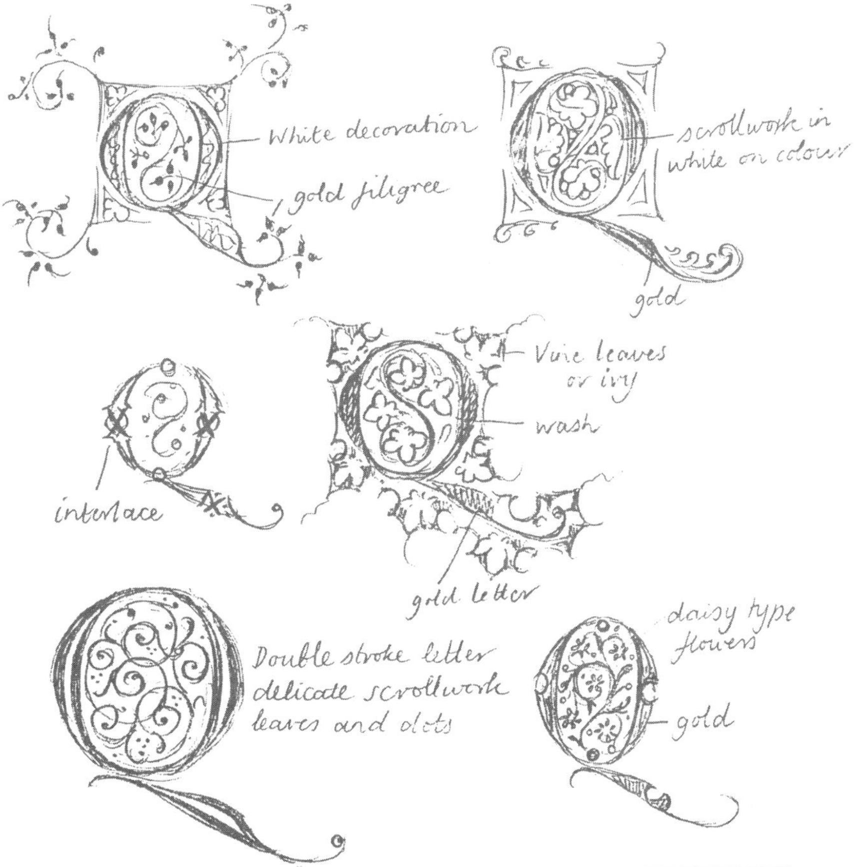

White decoration
gold filigree

scrollwork in white on colour
gold

Vine leaves or ivy
wash
gold letter

interlace

Double stroke letter
delicate scrollwork
leaves and dots

daisy type flowers
gold

THE FINAL COLOR ROUGH

The option eventually selected is a square design, broken by the tail, which includes vine motifs outside as well as inside the letter. The triangular silhouette of the four leaves placed around the O form of the Q makes up the corners of the square. The outside curves of the Q are angled, and the tail is given extra weight. Preliminary color choices are made: gold for the letterform with mauve and green decoration.

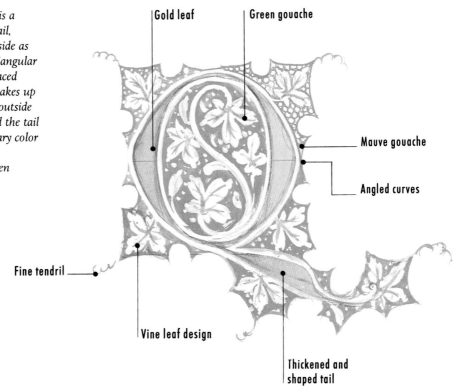

Gold leaf

Green gouache

Mauve gouache

Angled curves

Fine tendril

Vine leaf design

Thickened and shaped tail

1 With the tracing paper firmly taped in position, an accurate pencil tracing is made of the outlines of the final design. The outlines are drawn on the reverse side of the paper in a soft pencil.

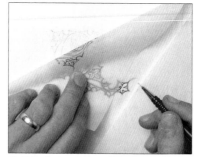

2 The design is transferred onto the chosen paper by placing the prepared tracing in position right side up. The outlines are drawn over again with a hard pencil so that the marks on the underside are transferred.

3 Gum ammoniac is applied to the letterform with a fine brush. The brush needs to be rinsed frequently in hot water to prevent the gum from clogging it. Breathing over the surface before the gold is applied restores tackiness.

4 Narrow strips of gold leaf are placed on the letterform, gold side down. The backing sheet is removed after rubbing through it to adhere the gold to the gum ammoniac.

5 All parts of the letterform are covered in gold leaf, and the final piece of backing sheet is removed.

6 The gold is burnished with a special burnishing tool through glassine paper. Tracing paper could be substituted. Afterward, any loose gold leaf is brushed away with a soft brush.

7 Sufficient quantities of the chosen colors of gouache are mixed to finish the job. The color is carefully applied with a fine sable brush.

8 For the final version, it is decided to use a muted green for the decoration inside the counter.

9 The last elements to be completed are the fine tendrils that extend from the corners of the design.

Gallery

The design and execution of illuminated letters brings together a variety of skills that the beginning calligrapher needs to develop. Not only are you concerned with the letterform itself, but also with the relationship of your illustration design to the letter and the work as a whole. Carefully select colors to enhance balance between letterform and decoration. The examples on this page show a variety of approaches.

I LAY AMONG PTERIS AQUILINA — Mark Van Stone

In this rendering of a 19th-century text (above), medieval-style illumination has been used.

VERSAL CONCERTINA BOOK — Donald Jackson

These elegant compressed versals (above) show how a traditional letterform can be used in a contemporary context.

MEDIEVAL STYLE ILLUMINATION — Mark Van Stone

This Latin text (left) is written and decorated in the style of the Lindisfarne Gospels. The watercolor decoration uses traditional Celtic knotwork motifs and the following text is written in ink in insular half-uncials.

Once you have mastered the basic letterforms, the scripts here and on the following pages will enable you to extend your calligraphic repertoire.

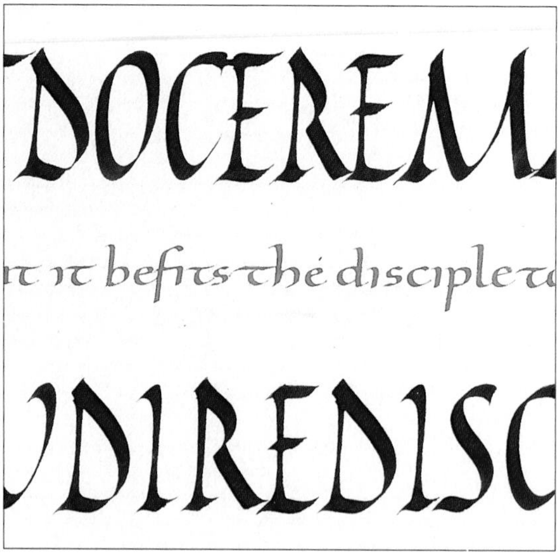

RUSTICA

Rustic capitals were at their height of popularity from the fourth to sixth centuries A.D. for manuscript writing, but examples of the script dating from the second century have been found. In modern calligraphy there are many uses for these stately letterforms.

Letter height: 7 nib widths.
Pen angle: 60°–90°. Some letters require twisting the pen.
O form: Oval.
Slant: 5° to the right.
Stroke number, order, and direction: As annotated on alphabet.
Speed: Slow.
Serifs: Slightly curved slab foot serifs.

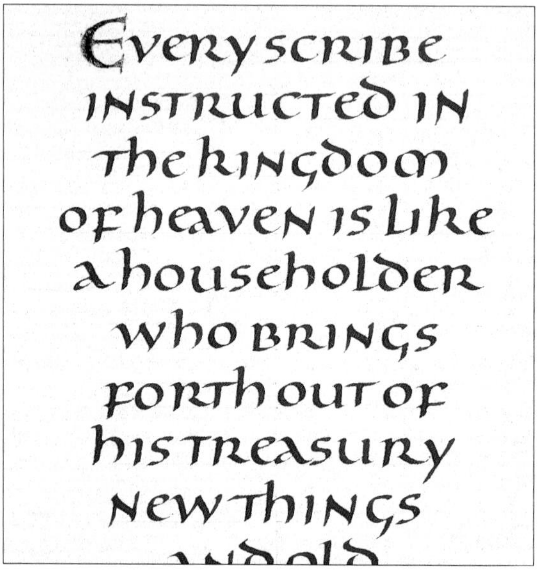

ROMAN UNCIAL

This majuscule (capital) script was in widespread use from the third to the ninth centuries A.D. Its forms were influenced by both Greek and Roman precedents. The version illustrated here is known as angled-pen uncial and is more suited than some other forms for contemporary use.

Letter height: X height 3½ nib widths, some letters extend above and below 2 nib widths more.
Pen angle: 20°.
O form: Slightly extended circle.
Slant: None.
Stroke number, order and direction: As annotated on alphabet.
Speed: Moderate.
Serifs: Simple hooks.

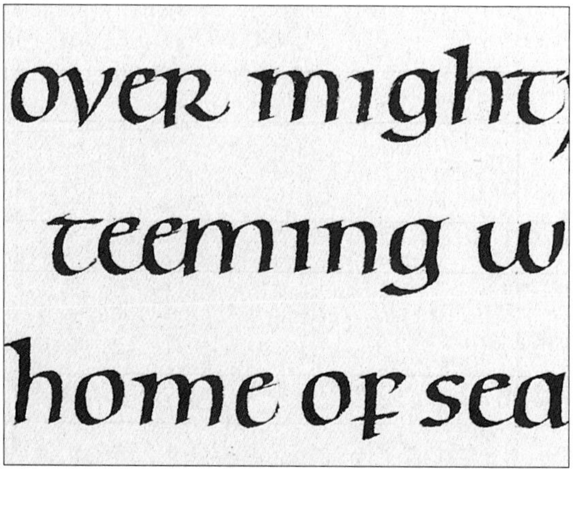

HALF UNCIAL

Dating from the sixth century A.D., this script was most beautifully written in England and Ireland as illustrated by the Insular half uncials shown here.

Letter height: X height 3–4 nib widths, ascenders and descenders 1½–2 nib widths more.
Pen angle: 0°.
Slant: None.
Stroke number, order, and direction: As annotated on alphabet.
Speed: Moderately slow.
Serifs: Club-shaped and built up.

CAROLINGIAN

The Carolingian minuscule is a flowing bookhand that developed during the late eighth century. It was accompanied by Roman versal or uncial capitals. It is a favorite script for contemporary manuscript books.

Letter height: *X height 3 nib widths, ascenders and descenders 4 nib widths.*
Pen angle: *30°.*
O form: *Slightly extended circle.*
Slant: *5°–10° to the right.*
Stroke number, order, and direction: *As annotated on alphabet.*
Speed: *Moderate.*
Serifs: *Simple hooks.*

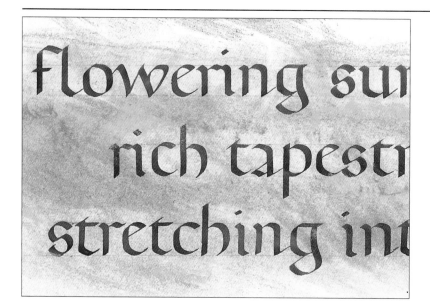

ROTUNDA MINUSCULE

This rounded Gothic script of Southern Europe was in use during the 13th to 15th centuries and was particularly popular in Italy.

Letter height: *X height 4 nib widths, ascenders and descenders 2 nib widths more.*
Pen angle: *30°.*
O form: *Squared-off circle.*
Slant: *None.*
Stroke number, order, and direction: *As annotated on alphabet.*
Speed: *Fairly slow.*
Serifs: *Squared serifs for some stroke beginnings and flattened endings to many vertical strokes achieved by turning the nib to an angle of 0° at the bottom of a stroke.*

SHARPENED ITALIC

This angular form of italic dates from the 15th century. It was developed in Italy alongside the more rounded versions of the script. Like all italics, it may be joined or unjoined and can be plain (as shown here) or flourished.

Letter height: *X height 5 nib widths, ascenders and descenders 4 nib widths.*
Pen angle: *45°.*
O form: *Sharpened oval.*
Slant: *5°–12° to the right.*
Stroke number, order, and direction: *As annotated on alphabet.*
Speed: *Moderate to fast.*
Serifs: *Sharpened.*

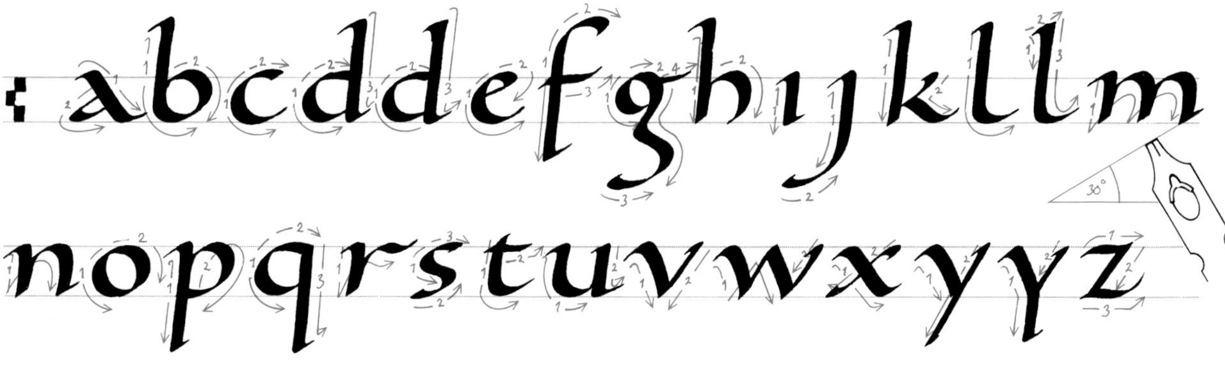
abcddefghijkllm
nopqrstuvwxyyz
30°

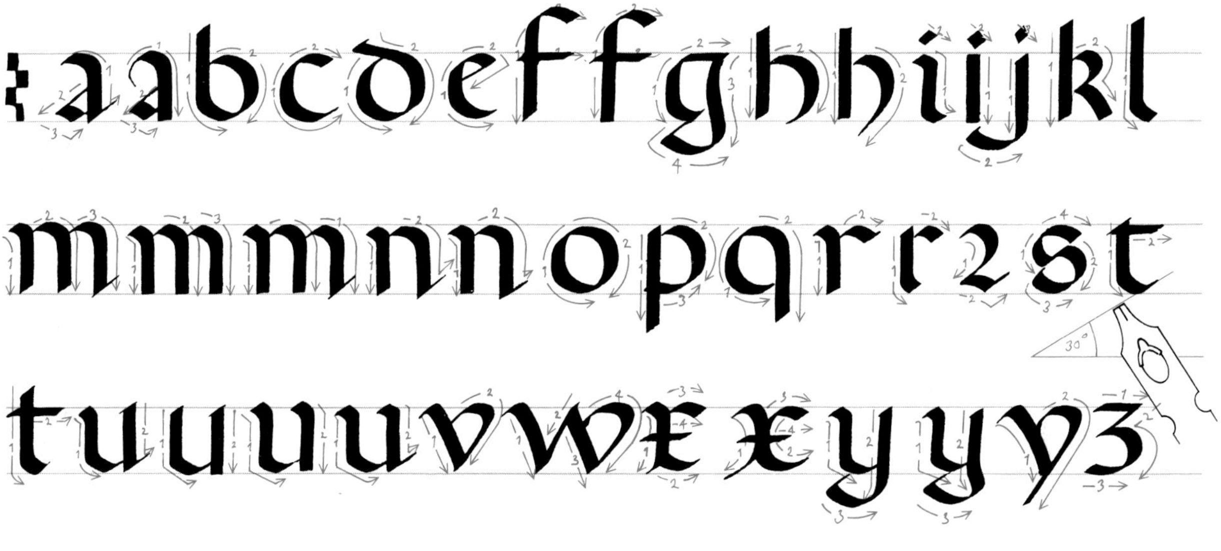
aabcdeffghhiijkl
mmmmnnopqrrrst
tuuuuvwxxyyyz
30°

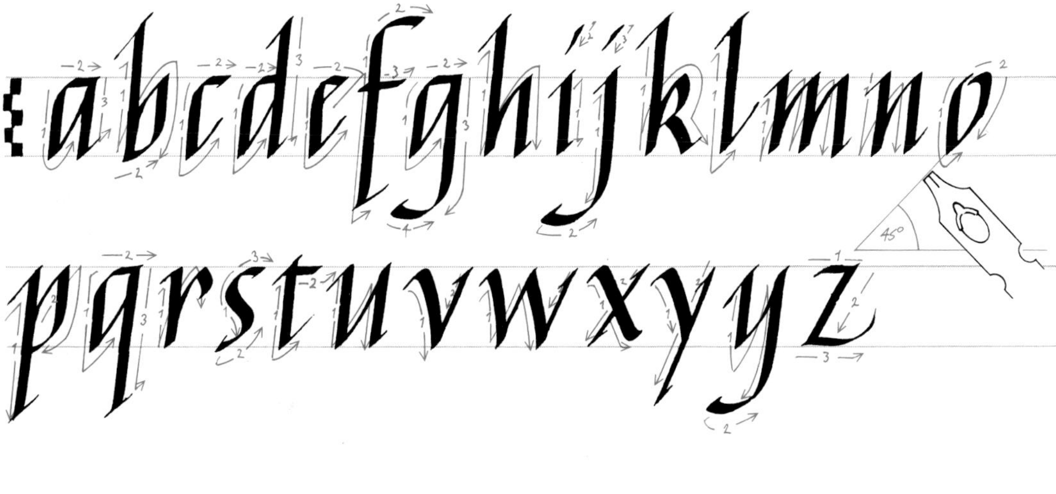
abcdefghijklmno
pqrstuvwxyyz
45°

Index

Credits

The publishers would like to thank all the calligraphers who submitted work for inclusion in the book and in particular the following who designed and produced the main projects in Part 5: **Lorraine Brady** (Letterhead); **John Neilson** (Poster and Manuscript book); **Timothy Noad** (Illuminated letter); **Penny Price** (Concertina book). The Invitation and Decorative border are by **Gaynor Goffe**. The Poetry broadsheet is by **Anna Ravenscroft**.

In addition, the publishers would like to thank the following: the Archer Press for printing the Letterhead; William Day (Engravers) Ltd for printing the Invitation; Hazel Bell for compiling the index; Karyn Gilman; David Kemp and Jane Royston for invaluable additional assistance.

Unless otherwise indicated, all calligraphic examples are by the authors.

Key: top (t); center (c); below (b); left (l); right (r).

8 Anna Ronchi. 9 John Nash (t); The Board of Trinity College Dublin (l); Donald Jackson (b). 10 V & A Museum (t); Joan Pilsbury (b). 11 Reproduced by kind permission of Mrs Andrew Johnston. 12 Magnus Astrom. "Feuerharfe" by Yvan Goll from *Dichtungen*, ed. C. Goll (Hermann Luchterhand Verlag, 1960). © Yvan Goll. Reproduced by permission of Argon Verlag, Berlin (t); Florian Kynman. "The Shield of Achilles" from *Collected Poems* by W H Auden (Faber & Faber, 1991). © W H Auden. Reproduced by permission of Faber & Faber (UK), Random House (USA) (b). 13 Ewan Clayton. "Spring's Firebird" by Rumi from *Love's Fire* translated by Andrew Harvey (Jonathan Cape, 1988). © Andrew Harvey. Reproduced by permission of Random Century Group (UK), Aitken, Stone and Wylie (USA) (t); Julia Vance (b). 22 Gareth Colgan. 45 Teresa Dunstone (br). 52 Gareth Colgan. 53 Liz Burch. 54 British Library. 55 Joan Pilsbury. 64 Angela Swann. 65 Claire Secrett. 76 John Neilson. 78 Bodleian Library, Oxford (t); Joan Pilsbury (b). 83 Gareth Colgan. 92 Louise Donaldson. 93 Liz Burch. 104 Paivi Vesanto. 105 Julia Vance. From *North* by Seamus Heaney (Faber & Faber, 1978). © Seamus Heaney. Reproduced by permission of Faber & Faber (UK) and Farrar, Strauss & Giroux (USA). 108 Paivi Vesanto. 112 Lawrence R. Brady. 114 Bodleian Library, Oxford 122–123 Anna Ravenscroft. 129 Anna Ravenscroft. 131 Anna Ravenscroft. 137 Angela Hickey (t); Timothy Noad (l); Bonnie Leah (br). 141 Bonnie Leah (t); Christopher Haanes (tr); Georgia Deaver (l); Elizabeth Rounce (bl). 145 Louise Donaldson (l); Janet Mehigan (r). 146 Nancy R. Leavitt (tl); Julia Vance (b); Paivi Vesanto (r). 147 Sheila Waters. "Tor House" from *The Selected Poetry of Robinson Jeffers* (Random House, 1959) © Robinson Jeffers. Reproduced by permission of W. W. Norton & Co (t); Gillian Hazeldine. From the *Exter Riddle Book* translated by Kevin Crossley-Holland (The Folio Society, 1978). © Kevin Crossley-Holland. Reproduced by permission of The Folio Society and Kevin Crossley-Holland. 151 Jenny Kavarana (l & b); Louise Donaldson (t). 155 Mary Noble (t); Anne Irwin; Patricia Lovett (b). 156–161 From *Strong Tea* by John B. Keane. Reproduced by permission of The Mercier Press, Cork. 160 Hazel Dolby (t); Kate Ridyard. From *Selected Poems* translated by Anthony Kerrigan (Jonathan Cape, 1970). © Reproduced by permission of Random Century Group (b). 161 Monica Dengo (t); Suzanne Moore (l); Joan Pilsbury (r). 165 Carina Westling (t); Joan Pilsbury and Wendy Westover (l); Gaynor Goffe (r). 169 Mark Van Stone (t & l); Donald Jackson (r). 170 Gareth Colgan. 171 Gareth Colgan (t); Lorraine Brady (b). 172 Louise Donaldson (t); Kate Ridyard (b).

While every effort has been made to acknowledge all copyright holders, Quarto would like to apologize if any omissions have been made.